THE HIGH

Directed by Kenneth White, t.　　　　　　　　series will follow the high line of Scottish and world culture, as seen by one of the most acute and comprehensive minds working today, the author of a considerable body of work (essay, prose, poetry), and a European intellectual of the highest order, from 1983 to 1996 holder of the Chair of Twentieth-Century Poetics at the Sorbonne.

The first book in the series, *On the Atlantic Edge*, comprises the three lectures White delivered in the Highlands and Islands in the autumn of 2005, as holder of the first Hi-Arts International Fellowship, along with his Edinburgh International Book Festival lecture on 'World Writing'.

Consisting mainly of relatively short books, the series will continue at a reasonable rate, finely designed and produced by Sandstone Press, each volume carrying a cover image from Highland-based artist Wendy Sutherland. Peter Urpeth, who provides the foreword to this first volume, is Writing Development Co-ordinator for the Highlands and Islands of Scotland with Hi-Arts, and as such was instrumental in initiating and organizing Kenneth White's 2005 lecture tour.

By the same author
(selected list)

Letters from Gourgounel, narrative
London, Jonathan Cape, 1966.
Travels in the Drifting Dawn, narrative
Edinburgh and London, Mainstream Publishing, 1989.
The Blue Road, narrative
Edinburgh and London, Mainstream Publishing, 1990.
Pilgrim of the Void, narrative
Edinburgh and London, Mainstream Publishing, 1992.
Van Gogh and Kenneth White, an encounter,
Paris, Flohic Éditions, 1994.
Coast to Coast, interviews
Glasgow, Open World Editions and Mythic Horse Press, 1996.
On Scottish Ground, selected essays
Edinburgh, Polygon, 1998.
House of Tides, narrative
Edinburgh, Polygon, 2000.
Geopoetics : Place, Culture, World, essay
Glasgow, Alba Editions, 2003.
Open World, Collected Poems 1960-2000
Edinburgh, Polygon, 2003.
The Wanderer and his Charts, essays
Edinburgh, Polygon, 2004.
Across the Territories, narrative
Edinburgh, Polygon, 2004.

Recorded poetry

Into the White World, two cassettes of poems readings
Scotsoun, 13 Ashton Rd, Glasgow G12 8SP, 1992.

On Kenneth White's work :

Grounding a world, essays by various authors, the St Andrews
University Symposium
Glasgow, Alba Editions, 2005.
Contains complete bibliography and biography.

KENNETH WHITE

ON THE ATLANTIC EDGE

A Geopoetics Project

THE HIGHLINER SERIES

Sandstone Press Ltd
Highland, Scotland

THE HIGHLINER SERIES

ON THE ATLANTIC EDGE

First published 2006 in Great Britain by Sandstone Press Ltd
PO Box 5725, One High Street, Dingwall, Ross-shire, IV15 9WJ

ISBN-10: 1-905207-08-5
ISBN-13 : 978-1-905207-08-4

Designed and typeset in Dutch
by River Design, Edinburgh

Printed and bound in the European Union.

*The three lectures from the HI~Arts International Fellowship were
commissioned with the financial support of Scottish Arts Council and
Highlands and Islands Enterprise.*

HI~ARTS

www.sandstonepress.com

CONTENTS

FOREWORD

It was very gratifying to learn that the three lectures Kenneth White delivered in the Highlands and Islands at the end of 2005, as part of the inaugural HI~Arts International Fellowship, were to form the main body of the first book in the new Highliner Series he is to direct for Sandstone Press. It is also entirely appropriate that the three Highlands and Islands lectures are joined in this book by a lecture given at the Edinburgh International Book Festival, for all four lectures specifically question fundamental issues in Scottish culture and provide new space for the rigourous search for similarly fundamental answers. But don't think that this is simply another book about Scottish history or literature. White's lectures provide both specific content and an indicative method that is global and plural in its potential application.

For HI~Arts, the appointment of Kenneth White as its first International Fellow was both a great honour for the organisation, and an obvious choice. For many years White lived like Joyce and Beckett, away from his first home but not in exile, and like them achieved significant recognition in a wider space than that of his homeland. As poet and thinker, working from the culture before him in Glasgow and in Scottish and British culture in general, White has developed a body of work which, via poem, waybook and essay, has grown to become world-encompassing, global in reach and application and multi-faceted in delivery. The sheer scope of his cultural and philosophical imagination distinguishes White from almost all of his contemporaries in both the Anglo-American and the

Continental contexts. His work ranges across cultures and disciplines, conventions and hierarchies.

Kenneth White responded to the award of the Fellowship by further development of the Geopoetics Project in the context of the North. In October 2005 he delivered a series of three lectures in Ullapool, Inverness and at Kirkwall, Orkney. Over three days, it became clear, as indeed it has always been clear from his public appearances, despite consistent attempts by a certain entrenched establishment to misrepresent and obfuscate his writings, that there was very significant demand for and response to his work. Indeed, over the last decade, White's work has begun to make an increasing impact on the UK, which is bound to expand, from the UK out into other English-speaking areas. The audiences at the lectures were not comprised solely of academics, nor even, however numerous they were, of writers and artists, but of people from all walks of life looking for ideas going beyond the framework of standardized cultural production. It is an indication of the plurality and extent of White's work that it speaks to such a diverse audience.

The publication of these lectures is an indication of the bold vision and ambition of Sandstone Press as an emerging literary publisher, and it only remains for me to wish all success to this Highliners Series at Sandstone Press as well of course to White's continuing work in general.

Peter Urpeth
Writing Development Co-ordinator
HI~Arts

PART ONE:

THE FUNDAMENTAL QUESTION

WHAT IS WORLD WRITING?

(The Edinburgh International Book Festival Lecture, August 21st 2005)

PROLOGUE

Good evening, all. I say it every year and it's always true: it's a pleasure to be back in Edinburgh at the International Book Festival.

I think most people in this hall tonight are aware of what I've been trying to do on this platform over the past few years. I've been attempting to raise fundamental questions – about culture, about literature, concerning a specific territory, Scotland (with potential extrapolations to other areas) – and I've been proposing some fundamental answers.

Not so long ago, in fact yesterday, for political-historical reasons which I think everyone is now aware of, Scotland was, culturally, a provincial backwater. I'm not talking about individuals, who will pursue good work and enhance their own lives whatever the ambiance, I'm talking about a general context, and a coordination, or lack of it. It was into this context that MacDiarmid arrived, with his ideas of a Scottish Renaissance. The man, whom I liked and appreciated highly, drove himself hoarse with vociferation and built up a mass of work that never reached complete coherence and was marked by a lop-sided gigantism.

Scotland is no longer a provincial backwater. Some time ago, it joined, at least great sections of it, the international mainstream. Its eye was on what a friend of mine, resident in Leith, calls the crap-market. To quote my friend, Scotland was saying to itself it could provide just as good crap as anywhere else, and maybe even better. Which it proceeded to do. With some success.

It was into this context I came along, with other ideas, other perspectives, saying this 'success' wasn't enough, that what it entailed was not only an absence of cogent actuality, but a coagulated accumulation of nonentity. What I wanted to do, along with others here in Scotland, (a lot has been going on, more or less subterraneanly, more or less marginally, but without coordination), was work at what I think of as a third movement, that is, get something going in Scotland outside a crap-market context marked by myopic positivism, mushy populism, fumbling empiricism, jovial Johnbullism, and various other similar ingredients.

I've entitled my talk this year: What is World Writing? As can be seen from the title of my collected poems, *Open World*, 'world' is a key-word in my mind and work.

What about *writing* a world? That is the question.

1. WRITING A WORLD

By the 'world writing' of my title, I don't simply mean a panoramic view of the writing done all over the world. Most of what is called 'creative writing' done all over the world today is insignificant when it isn't pernicious. I'm a partisan of what

Goethe, back at the end of the eighteenth century, called 'world literature' (*Weltliteratur*), meaning by that the idea that no demanding, expanding mind could be satisfied any longer with any national literature and that it was necessary to look beyond the borders. Since no one can know all the languages of the world, that meant translation. Some of the great transformations of culture have come via translation. I'm thinking of the work done on Indian texts at Tchang-an in China in the seventh century, or the translation into Spanish of Greek, Persian and Coptic texts by Arabs and Jews in twelfth-century Toledo. There was a strong sense there of what was needed. But nowadays the mere fact that a book is published in thirty languages is no sign in itself of value. The book may have belonged to the shelves of crapology in its local context, it now belongs to the shelves of universal crapology, that's all. No mind is advanced or expanded one whit by this activity. On the contrary.

What I mean by world-writing, while including Goethe's 'world-literature', goes further.

What I mean by world-writing is writing that *opens space*.

But that's only a preliminary definition.

Before moving out, let's look at the world as it is around us.

The world is where we're enclosed in a category, a social function, and work according to a more or less limited code. Of course there can be satisfaction in this, at least some of the time, when the routine doesn't run down to fuggy sluggishness or speed up to harassed agitation. Whatever the social context, we feel, we know, that it leaves out a lot of our 'being' (I put the word in inverted commas because you have to be careful with it - it can lead you up all kinds of garden paths and into dead ends).

5

That 'being' of ours consists most of the time of half-thoughts, confused sentiment, a cinematic rush of dreams and fantasies, with, in the background, a vague or nagging sensation of frustration, deep discontent. This is the world Wordsworth has in mind when he says in his poem that 'the world is too much with us', that we 'lay waste our powers' in 'getting and spending', and are 'out of tune'. This is the world we want to get rid of when we express the desire to 'get out of ourselves', 'forget ourselves', 'get away from it all'. We do manage to do this, momentarily, via some form of amusement, or with the use of some kind of drug. Then, there are religions that propose 'another world', and spiritualities that offer some kind of vapoury fuminess in place of a world. And there are ideologies that promise to replace the cacotopia (from the Greek *kakos:* poor, vile – shitty) with a utopia, that always turns, if no fundamental work is done in time, into just another kind of cacotopia.

There's a literature that corresponds to the cacotopian context I've just evoked. It is the great mass of literature. It can take various forms. I don't intend to go into them all, but will list some. There's the literature of fantasy, to enjoy which you have to be infantile or senile. There's a literature that reflects the situation, providing a kind of mirror satisfaction, pushing it at times up into the dramatic, or, when this has been played out, down into the crudely pathological. There's a literature that sets a plot in it, with a beginning, a middle, and an end, which gives a kind of elementary Q.E.D. satisfaction (the simplest form here is the detective novel). You can interpret the context in political terms as, say, bourgeois, and offer a straight-from-the-pavement proletarian alternative, which, in fact, is only the obverse side of the same coin.

All of this is *literature*.

But, over the past couple of centuries, there have been attempts to get out of all this literature, and get down to a radical *writing* (allied to a radical thinking) based on another conception of *world*.

You can see the first stirrings in Romanticism, especially continental Romanticism. There you have Novalis in his notebooks saying that real writing hasn't yet begun, and Hölderlin in his book *Hyperion* (the account of a man with hyper-desires) saying: 'What you're looking for is a world'. It was the first crisis of modernity, that modernity which was increasingly separating subject from object, the human being from the external environment, leaving the citizen without a live world to live in. Since that first crisis, there has been a lot of radical criticism, criticism of systems of society, philosophy and literature, exploration of new ways of living, thinking and writing. Any social or literary criticism that continues blandly making its comments sublimely unaware of these movements is beside the point. Likewise any history. World-writing isn't history (though it can use history, as it uses other arts and sciences), it is poetics and, more specifically, geopoetics.

What we're concerned with ('we', let's say, the waybreakers), is a reformulation of premises, an affirmation of new axioms. I've gone into all this in my essays – *The Wanderer and his Charts*, for example – so will provide here only the merest outline.

Nietzsche distinguishes three types of creativity: tragedy (where you present the pathology of society), satire (where you make fun of the normal, normalized context), and, most difficult, most significant, also most exciting and most pleasurable of all, *world-making*, where you move into another field. Husserl, in his attempt to get beyond the subject-object split, presents the 'transcendental ego' before entering the land of phenomenology. Heidegger, in his book with Fink on Heraclitus, describes the human being as 'world-making' (*weltbildend*), then breaks down any fixed edifice of world, speaking rather of perpetual 'worldification', saying, in actively verbal, non-substantial terms: 'there never is a world, but there is worlding' (*Welt ist nie, sondern weltet*). This is sensitive ground, subtle territory.

With this kind of thinking in mind, we can take a new look at language. What I presented earlier as 'world' is contained in the Germanic root of the word: *wer-alt*, a 'time of man', a socio-historical context, no more than that. But there have been other conceptions of 'world'. The Greek word *kosmos* indicates a harmonious whole. In the romance languages, *mundo, mondo, monde*, have, radically, an aesthetic connotation. This is manifested nowadays, and it is significant, only negatively, as in the French *immonde*, which means ugly, loathsome, or in the English *mundane*, which means ordinary, boring. If we go even further back into Indo-European, we can see a relationship between the Latin word for man, *homo*, and the word for earth, *humus*.

My mention of Indo-European brings me to the East-West thing. Ever since Romanticism, there has been awareness in the advanced thought of the West that the East, which became a separate world at a historical point, has preserved elements of a thinking that the West has forgotten. This doesn't mean, at least in my conception of things, 'conversion' to anything, but it does mean a prolonged conversation. Bringing in, for example, notions and practices of liberation of the mind from dualism, and deconditioning of the self from the codes and constraints of the 'normal world' I began by evoking. Or the statement one can find in the *Diamond sutra*: 'The world they live in isn't the real world. That's why they call it "the world".' Or the distinction to be found in Japanese aesthetics between writing that 'has a world' and writing that 'doesn't have a world'.

The definition I myself have come to – and I don't impose it arbitrarily on the language, as has been said here in Scotland, it stems from all the investigations I've just presented – is this: a world arises from the contact between the human mind and 'what's out there'. When the contact, the relationship, is sensitive, intelligent, subtle, you have a world in the full sense of the word. When the contact is brutal, stupid, ignorant, you have . . . cacotopia.

I've worked at all this a long time, and the results are there in my books, in various forms. But, before coming back to them, since we're here, in Scotland, a country I have wanted to work with, and in Edinburgh, a city with which I have strong affiliations, I want to talk with you here tonight about one of Edinburgh's, one of Scotland's high cultural moments, and about a lot of Scottish thinking and writing done there, which is my background, and which I've always lived with.

2. THE EDINBURGH FERMENTATION

Twenty-five centuries ago, three men: a politician, Pericles; an architect, Phidias; and a poet, Sophocles, met on the heights of

Athens with the idea of giving a radiant form to the city and making it 'the school of Greece'. The result was the architectural complex of the Acropolis, and, back of the architecture, a *paideia*, a whole system of poetic and philosophical education making for a live, brilliant culture.

Edinburgh, in the eighteenth century, took this as a model: 'the Athens of the North'.

Athens no longer corresponds to this image. Neither does Edinburgh. Look what's happened, hideously, to Princes Street. Go up the Calton Hill and have a look over the city skyline. One is reminded of Cockburn's 1849 pamphlet: *A Letter to the Lord Provost on the Best Ways of Spoiling the Beauty of Edinburgh*.

Anyway, my theme tonight is not architecture, it is writing, and what I have in mind is the notion of *paideia* (thought, poetics, education, culture) of which, in the Greek conception of things, architecture was to be the house.

A few months ago in Paris, Edinburgh was nominated by UNESCO a 'City of Literature'. Although some of the contemporary material put forward to confirm Edinburgh's claim was more embarrassing than anything else, I supported that claim, thinking, along with a possible future, mainly of the city's past and, principally, of that moment known as the Enlightenment.

What I want to do in this section of my lecture is give a quick overview of that Enlightenment movement, which is where I started.

The highliners are David Hume, Adam Smith and James Hutton.

Born in Edinburgh on April 26th, 1711, Hume went up to the city college to study law. But, as he says in the little autobiographical essay contained in his *Enquiry concerning Human Understanding*, 'I found an unsurmountable Aversion to every thing but the pursuits of Philosophy and General Learning'. To these pursuits he devoted all his time, ploughing across miles of muddy metaphysics in the search for Truth, not finding it, only succeeding in driving his physical constitution to wretched illness, at which time he had recourse to a doctor, who recommended easing up a bit.

He decided to leave what he felt as the narrow precincts and calvinistic atmosphere of Edinburgh, for France. All his life he was to be moving, if not in body, at least in mind, between Scotland and the country across the water. In France, back there at his first move, after passing through Paris, he ended up at the country town of La Flèche in Anjou, where he could live cheaply, enjoy pleasant wine, and get on quietly with his work and thinking, having access for books to the library of a Jesuit college in the town. Even in his mad metaphysical days, he had sometimes had the impression that 'a new scene of thought' was opening for him: not the kingdom of Truth, but a whole new mindscape beyond belief, ideology, opinion. It was this mindscape that began really opening out in the book he wrote in France: *A Treatise of Human Nature*. When it appeared, at London, in 1739, it did not receive much attention, because nobody knew how to handle it. In Scotland, that Scotland whose narrowness he loathed, but to which he had returned because his friends lived there, Hume had all the Common Sense philosophers, Thomas Reid at the head of the pack, yelping at his heels, condemning the book as immoral, atheistical, extravagant, paradoxical, dogmatic and rank with intellectual pride. Who was this fellow so damnably conceited that he would throw out, as so much rotten and dead thought, all the most solid intuitions of humanity and the foundations of its institutions such as belief in a benevolent God and teleological design in the Universe?

Hume took it all in silence. To get his ideas across in a more gradual way, also to make a living, he tried for the Chair of Ethics and Pneumatical Philosophy at Edinburgh, where he got blackballed, then for the chair of Logic at Glasgow, where he got blackballed all over again. The job he finally managed to obtain was as librarian at the Library of Advocates in Edinburgh, where, even in this quiet haven, he got severely censured for bringing in books from the Continent that were considered as subversive of correct thinking, good opinion, established existence.

He continued to write his own books, reducing his radical scepticism to palatable proportions in essays (*Essays Moral and Political*) or in histories. In his *History of Great Britain*, he suggests that the 'enthusiasm' and 'fanaticism' of the Reformation was worse in its effects than Papal superstition, and that the 'inwards life' of Protestantism had led to horrible catacombs of hypocrisy and nightmarish fantasy.

What sense Hume himself had of an '*outwards* life' was not great. Having pushed his thought, extravagantly, right to the limits, while keeping its radical scope and scape at the back of his head, expressing it discreetly at times, he chose to live an affable social life, regaling his friends at his lodgings with home-made punch and dishes he cooked up himself. I have known other radical sceptics who have adopted similar tactics. Sometimes I think they are right, but only sometimes. A radical sceptic myself in many ways, I still feel the impulse (pleasure rather than need) to keep in touch with the outside and act outwards.

One of Hume's closest friends was Adam Smith, known glibly as 'the founder of modern economy', because he made a study of liberal capitalism in *The Wealth of Nations*, but whose scope was in fact much wider than that of the expounder-apologist of liberalism. The man wrote essays also on cosmology and right up to his death he had in mind a vast study that would comprise all the different branches of literature and philosophy, not simply in a panoramic way, but in a synthetizing way, and with an attempt to get at first principles. It's true that in the *Wealth* Smith gets almost totally absorbed in the technical mechanics of the new economy, and brushes off any deep doubts he has with a vague belief in an 'invisible hand' that will work things out for the best, but even there we can find criticism of the excessive division of labour that was to develop into Taylorism, Fordism, and a lot of other 'progressive' schemes: 'The man whose whole life is spent performing a few simple operations', he says, and who has, therefore 'no occasion to exert his understanding', becomes 'as stupid and ignorant as it is possible for a human creature to become'. But for Smith's social criticism, it's to other texts we have to turn.

When he held the Chair of Moral Philosophy at Glasgow (I attended its classes myself a couple of hundred years later, well aware of Smith in the background, because *The Wealth of Nations* was on my father's not extensive, but significant bookshelves), his course was divided into four parts: the foundations of religion; ethics; justice; institutions (commerce and finance). This led to his book *A Theory of Sentiments*. In that book, Smith studied the rise of big business and industry from a distance, looking askance at those 'enormous and operose machines' that 'produce a few trifling conveniences'. That was two centuries ago, what would he say today? In another text of the same period, he has this: 'In a commercial society such as England or lowland Scotland, the minds of men are contracted and rendered incapable of elevation, education is despised or at least neglected, and heroic spirit is almost utterly extinguished.' He concluded that text with this: 'To remedy these defects would be an object worthy of serious attention.'

A lot of debate went on in Edinburgh on such questions. It tended to take the form of a whole series of dialectical pairs such as: unionism and nationalism, royalism and republicanism, order and anarchy, religion and atheism, reason and feeling, progress and primitivism, nature and culture, society and solitude.

Let me just evoke some particular instances.

As from 1707, there was a strong Unionist line in the North, as expressed, for example, by Alexander Wedderburn in *The Edinburgh Review* in 1755: 'If countries have their ages with respect to improvement, North Britain may be considered as in a state of early youth, guided and supported by the more mature strength of its kindred country.' In the minds of its adherents, what Unionism meant was a move from undeveloped crudeness and political immaturity to a constitutional stability based on rational utilitarianism, humdrum empiricism, and stubborn commercialism. I'm expressing it there in abstract terms. But back of this programme lay a politico-religious faith, the Puritan myth, as developed by Milton in the *Areopagitica* (God's revelations to the English) or by John Harrington in his *Oceana* of 1654, a hymn to political expansion and increase in the volume of trade, with England divinely designated as having a spiritual rôle to play on the world-scene. Britain hardly aspires to this kind of rôle today, except perhaps in its wackier areas. It is the United States that, again in its less intelligent areas, has forged ahead on this myth, with Britain in tow.

In Scotland, there was a counter-current to such a myth and such a programme. This counter-current started up in minds not only unconvinced that the Puritan Protestant was an anthropo-political model (seeing in him rather a hypocritical pervert), but interested in small republics, such as Venice, and in the possible growth of an organic culture based not on material interest but on what Adam Smith, before he got down to his cold analysis of industrial-capitalist mecanisms, called the 'heroic spirit'. It was a confused enough field at times, at times degenerating into coffee-room disputes or tavern brawls in which 'citizens' were opposed to 'clansmen', country Spartacists to towny Athenians, and contradictions were rife, even in one single mind.

Adam Ferguson, to take an example, was a Unionist but with reservations, and at the same time he was attracted to republicanism – but without ever going to the length of continental republicanism as expounded in France. When the Americans, inspired by French ideas, declared their Independence in 1776, it was as 'the extravagant plans of a Continental Republic' that Ferguson condemned that movement. In his *Essay on the History of Civil Society* of 1767, whose argument is based on the principle that the wealth of a nation is not to be measured by the size of its commerce and industry, but by its cultural, intellectual and ethical strength, he takes a long look at the progress of society from barbarism to business, from territorial warring to polite conversation, weighing up the pros and cons. If he recognizes progress, he also regrets values lost. Over against refined Athens, he sets the heroic spirit and rough honesty of Sparta; over against the socially constrained and commercially inclined cities of Edinburgh and Glasgow, he sets Gaelic culture, with its group solidarity, its unalienated freedom, and its poetry of place and space. He wonders if some kind of equilibrium might be obtained and sustained. To make up his mind about this, and because he was bored with the debating chambers, he decided to hole up, in distance and in silence, in his Edinburgh house, which came to be known as *Kamschatka*.

Another live mind in this field was that of James Stewart. For having been out, in an unconvinced kind of way, in the '45, with the 'wild Hielandmen', it was in exile on the continent, at various places – Paris, Angoulême, Brussels, Frankfurt and finally Tübingen – that he worked at his *Inquiry into the Principles of Political Oeconomy*. When it came out in 1767, this critical analysis of modern commercial society was branded in Britain as 'foreign'.

It was in fact on the Continent, in France, that all of these ideas were gathering head. It was there they had started up, with Rousseau's *Discourse on the Sciences and the Arts* at Dijon in 1750, that contained among other references, the specific invocation to Sparta (*'Ô, Sparte!'*) that was to be picked up, with local connotation and application, in Scotland, even to this day.

Along with the Spartan reference, Rousseau had in mind workers' communities in the Jura mountains, and he looked towards the constitution of a new republic in Corsica. But it was in France that the smouldering fire burst into flame.

The French revolution struck terror into Britain, making it react on all fronts, practically putting an end for years to any speculative thought, making minds lose the habit of it, which is why a Scottish Rousseauist like Robert Burns (dancing a desperate reel among his many contradictions) had such a hard time of it. Johnbullism was about to set in with a vengeance. On the continent, on the contrary, the Revolution was seen by republican thinkers as never having gone far enough, except in bloody confusion. In 1793, Robespierre was to make at the Assembly a declaration such as this: 'The French people and its representatives respect the liberty of all religions and prohibit none. They condemn the extravagance of the philosophers.' This was going back on all the advanced thinking of the age. Which is why the Marquis de Sade felt the need to bring out a pamphlet in defence of that philosophical extravagance and of political experiment: 'One more effort, citizens, if you want to be *really* republican.' The only man in Britain who had anything like this kind of vista of thought was David Hume, but he was keeping sceptically quiet, and epicureanly enjoying his oysters. In his *Dialogues concerning Natural Religion*, which he chose not to publish during his lifetime, he has this: 'Survey most nations and most ages. Examine the religious principles which have in fact prevailed in the world. You will scarcely be persuaded they are anything but sick men's dreams.'

It was maybe to get away from 'sick men's dreams' and

17

endless debates, that James Hutton turned to the rocks.

Were it not for the fact that so many people, and not only in the American Bible-belt, still seem to believe in some such weird cosmogonical scheme, it might seem incredible that as late as the middle of the nineteenth century, there were still minds in Britain willing to accept the declaration made in the seventeenth century, after considerable painstaking Biblical study, by the Irish ecclesiastic, James Ussher, in his *Annals of the World*, according to which God created the universe (for the benefit of humanity) in 4004 BC on the 22nd of October, which was a Saturday, 'at about 6 p. m.' Over against confabulations of this kind, Hutton has this: 'We are not to limit Nature with our imbecillity', and this: 'Let us open the book of Nature and read in her records.' Which is exactly what he did, expressing his awareness in strong rhythmic prose: 'The heights of our land are levelled with the shores; our fertile plains are formed from the ruins of the mountains; and those travelling materials are still pursued by the moving water, and propelled along the inclided surface of the earth. These moveable materials, delivered into the sea, cannot, for long continuance, rest upon the shore; for, by the agitation of the winds, the tides and currents, every moveable thing is carried farther and farther along the shelving bottom of the sea, towards the unfathomable regions of the ocean.'

This evocation of a great world-landscape, which is also a mindscape, brings me to the third section of my talk: my own work-field.

3. WORK IN PROGRESS

As I said, a lot of my own work has its background, and its humus, in the Scottish Enlightenment context I've just described. What I've tried to do over the years, in and out of Scotland, but always *with* Scotland, is work its various strands into a coherent whole, convert its dialectics into a poetics.

Anyone at all acquainted with my writings, whether in the form of essay or poem, or the territorial explorations of the waybook, will have seen the obvious, at least surface, connection between Hutton's work on the basic foundations and primary movements of the planet and the *general* field I finally worked out: geopoetics.

It was an early knowledge of Hutton's work that set me looking with a sharper eye and a more open mind along the shores of North Ayrshire and around the island of Arran. It was on the basis of Hutton's tectonics, concerned with the open structure of strata and the introduction into these open structures of all kinds of heterogeneous matter, this collocation of matter being later subjected to dislocation, fracturisation, all sorts of transference and translation, that I gradually derived a style of writing, let's say, employing the kind of linguistic shift I love, a *textonics*. From Hutton's investigation into 'the unknown region, that place of power and energy which we want to explore', I derived the notion of an exploratory, out-feeling poetics concerned with an undefined region or dimension, in a terrestrial context unencumbered by mythology, religion or metaphysics. Hutton's 'theory of the earth' I see as the bottom line of the Scottish Enlightenment, and I consider Hutton, along with Hume, the one cleaning the mind-works, the other getting at earth-knowledge, as the principal Scottish precursors of geopoetics. I speak there of two aspects, the earth-thing and the mind-thing, but in geopoetics they come together. Hume, in his *Dialogues*, has this, which might be taken as an epigraph to the whole geopoetic conception and movement: 'For aught we know, *a priori*, matter may contain the source, or spring, of order originating within itself, as well as the mind does.'

I trust that everyone in this hall will appreciate just how enormous that statement is.

Geopoetics is enormous, in the double sense of that word: it is vast in its scope, and it lies outside the norms. A lot of ways have led up to it, and a lot of ways can lead out from it. It is, potentially, culture-founding, world-making.

About his own investigations, Hutton has this: 'So great an idea may appear like a thing imaginary.' What is, in the first instance, enormous, e-normous, about this idea I am putting forward is that it is a thinking, a *pensation*, connected with what Laurence Sterne calls: 'the great sensorium of the world', that goes beyond all the compensations of the imaginary. In his book on Hutton published at Edinburgh in 1802, John Playfair develops Hutton's own statement so: 'Ages may be required to fill up the bold outline which Dr Hutton has traced with so masterly a hand.'

Ages have passed. A great deal of work has been done since those great Edinburgh days on geology and tectonics, as on all the other themes of dialectics I evoked. It's all of these I've tried to incorporate in my work, and in the theory-practice of geopoetics.

PART TWO:
NEW LIGHT ON THE NORTH
The Highlands and Islands Lectures

NORTH ATLANTIC INVESTIGATIONS
(Ullapool, October 29th 2005)

PROLOGUE

This is the first of three lectures devoted to cultural exploration in Scotland. These lectures will mean delving into history, looking at geography, re-examining the literary tradition – and opening up a new field of possibility on the basis of what I call geopoetics.

Before whaling into the open ocean and developing my theme, a word as to the notion of Atlantic Arc, which has come to the fore in recent years. Up here in Ullapool, we're at its northern edge, since it stretches from the southern tip of Portugal up to the Scottish archipelagoes.

The idea of the Atlantic Arc emerged from a meeting at Rennes, in Brittany, on September 8th, 1989. But it gathered full momentum at Faro, in Portugal, a month later (October 9th, 1989), when twenty-three European regions recognized that, facing out on to it, they shared a common space: the Atlantic, which had to a large extent shaped their destinies, and might provide a context in which to situate new intentions.

Olivier Guichard, one of the instigators of the idea, with Yvon Bourges, at Rennes, declared that those Euro-Atlantic regions were 'determined to enlarge the horizon of their perspectives', and Jean-Pierre Raffarin, due to become president of the Atlantic Arc Commission of the European Parliament, was to say: 'The Atlantic Arc has found its legitimacy – not that of a new political territory, but of a space for projects.'

A space for projects – that is something to my liking.

But if projects are going to be something other than politically blinkered or culturally half-baked, they need to have a basis – as broad a basis as possible, but at the same time sharp with specifics, making for a landing field liable to inspire interesting take-offs and long-lasting flights.

That's why I've chosen to entitle this series of lectures I'm to be doing in the Highlands and Islands region the Geopoetics Project, geopoetics having as its purpose to provide a basis for something like coherent and cogent culture in our time.

1. ELEMENTS OF ATLANTICITY

On our terraqueous globe, sea-mass stands to land-mass roughly in the proportion of 5 to 2.

Attempts have been made to see in this sphere of land and water, contracting from some original mobile molten mass, a logical shape, a geometrical tendency: the oceans and seas representing the faces of a tetrahedral, pyramidal form, the continents its rims. This theory tells more about a tendency of the human mind (marked by a more or less rational imagination) than about the actual reality, which is more moving and complex.

At the present moment, Wegener's theory of continental drift seems most adequate to that reality. Wegener posits the break-up of an early land-mass, Pangea, with continents (later theory extended these to tectonic plates) moving over the earth's crust owing to the presence of some force later identified as convective currents. What had first drawn Wegener's mind to the idea of the drift was that congruency between the shapes, across the Atlantic, of the West African coast and the Eastern coast of South America. It was the separation of those coasts that led to the influx of the Atlantic, a separation that is still continuing, with the Atlantic ocean slowly expanding.

Whatever be the origin and the explanation, what we have, phenomenologically, at the present juncture, is a sphere dividable into a northern and a southern hemisphere, with more land-mass in the North (land to sea in the proportion of 2 to 3), more sea-mass in the south (land to sea in the proportion of 1 to 4).

Looking at a globe, what strikes the eye most are coastlines. This area where land and water encounter each other is perhaps the most characteristic feature of our planet.

That is maybe why an old Gaelic text, *The Talk of the Two Scholars*, has this: 'The shore was always a place of revelation for the poets'. And why, centuries later, an essayist such as Emerson could write: 'The point of greatest interest is the place where land and water meet.' Here, he goes on to say, is 'the concentration of the vastitude, the form of the formless', stimulating in man both 'the cave of memory' and 'the house of reason'.

To live close to the sea and with the sea is to be aware of the biological origins of life. It is also to be aware of rhythms and patterns – tidal systoles and diastoles, wave-shapes and wave-movements, currents and winds, a changing meteorology, the multiple variations of a coastline –, and, with all that, to have a pervasive sense of chaos and cosmos, chaosmos.

This is the bottom line, the radical context, and any lasting, living, life-giving culture has to come back to it. It will be there in its art and in its poetry, in its thought, in its attitudes and in its actions.

Let's now zoom in on some detail.

By 9000 BC, the ice had so drawn north that the climate in our region was sub-arctic rather than arctic. Pine was coming in, along with earlier birch, willow, beech. By 7000 to 5000 BC, the climate was boreal, with oaks, hazel and alders. Between 5000 and 2000, it was becoming Atlantic, that is mild, and moist.

The first *strandloopers* (paleolithic beachcombers) who came roaming and ranging along the Atlantic coast, while looking for shellfish, were also getting the elements of this basic context written into their psyche.

When the megalith people, the Atlantic Stone folk, began to move up the Atlantic coast from Spain to Brittany and Britain, around 2000 BC, building their cromlechs, dolmens and tombs and raising their pillars, it would often be wave-patterns, sea-undulations they would chisel on their rocks – as in the tomb on the Isle of Goats in the Little Sea (*Mor Bihan*) of Brittany.

Leaving these people for the moment to continue their movements, let's look at how the Atlantic was seen by representatives of other cultures. For the Arabs, the Atlantic was 'the sea of darkness'. As for the Greeks, Pindar advised them never to venture out on to it, but always to stay inside the Pillars of Hercules – which is what even Ulysses did. It's only Dante, in Canto 26 of the *Inferno*, who has Ulysses voyage out into the unknown ('far as Morocco, far as Spain . . .until we could discern the marks that Hercules set in view that none should dare beyond'), only to have a storm rise 'out of that strange area' and wreck him.

Take now the Phoenicians, the 'red dye folk' (they liked dying fabrics with a purple-red colour they got from the shellfish *murex*). Little is known about them, even yet (classical sources stick mostly to stories about war, with a little love interest in between). But it was they who, nosing out from their ports on the shore of the Eastern Mediterranean: Tyre, Sidon, Byblos (where the first bibles, that is, books, came from), opened the way over to the west, past Crete, past Sicily, along the Moroccan coast, up to the Straits of Gibraltar, and out beyond, down the Atlantic coast of Africa, up by the coast of Portugal to the gulf of Gascony, to Brittany and Britain. They founded sea-cities, building them on rocky headlands, thus providing two ports, to be used according to wind and seasonal weather. But mainly they moved past islands and along shores, naming features as they went. It was these names, designating physical features, that Homer took over, making out of them gods and goddesses (Circe, Calypso, etc.), and making up stories. It took the French scholar, Victor Bérard, in the late nineteenth century, to read back of the stories and return to the original geographical document of the Phoenicians.

Homer, as has always to be stressed if we're going to 'atlanticize' culture, largely fictionalized and phantasized the Phoenician movement, but a Latin poet like Avienus, in his fourth century AD poem *Ora Maritima* ('Sea Shores'), had access to original documents that even Herodotus the great researcher did not know – which is why I felt the need to translate that poem from the Latin some years ago:

I've been gathering together the elements
of a pretty complex story
if you'll bear with me for a while
I'll give you the truth about these shores
truth with some sea-salt in it . . .

Original documents can be very exciting to the mind (more exciting than most literature), and not only exciting, but enlightening.

Another example.

For years now, among the maps that line the walls of my 'Atlantic Studio' on the north coast of Brittany, I've had the chart of the peregrinations of Pytheas as sketched out by Gaston Broche in his *Pythéas le Massaliote* (Paris, 1935), a book I have along with other Pytheana in my library. It shows the itinerary of this Atlantic traveller of the fourth century B.C. out from Marseilles, round Iberia, up the coast of Celtica, across to Britannia, up by the Hebrides and the Orkneys to Iceland, then across to Scandinavia and the Baltic: one of the most amazing trips in the history of exploration.

Pytheas's Marseilles was a Greek colony, which added to the intellectuality of Greece (the philosophical pedagogy of the Athenian city-state) the advantages of being on the edge, at the limits, away out there in the Western Mediterranean. In the hinterland of the port roamed those whom the Greeks called Keltoi, wild folk, barbarians – but interesting (for example, that whorling, whirling abstract art style) to somebody with an enquiring, outward-going mind like Pytheas.

As to the general environment of the times down there in the fourth century ante-Christian Mediterranean, Phoenicians, remember, had long been feeling their way out west from trading post to trading post. When the Greeks, hitherto, as we've seen, afeared of moving a step beyond the Pillars of Hercules, started at last to show signs of wanting to join the act, the Phoenicians tried to push them back, keep them out of the lucrative Atlantic business (tin, amber, gold). And those wild Kelts were threatening the whole Greco-Roman world, laughing at gods with human faces, showing no respect at all for what classical humanism had so laboriously built up. Unless the whole world was to end up in confused squabbling, in internecine warfare, it looked as if a new scheme of things was necessary.

That, I think (and I've lived with the ghost of this man a long time), was what was paramount in the mind of Pytheas.

It may be that he fitted out his own boat (was he the son of a trader, with a lot of sailing experience already to his credit?), but he may have used local boats for at least three reasons: less bother; possibility of confabbing with the natives in an ethnological kind of way; access to direct knowledge of particular areas from long-experienced local skippers.

It was going to be a long journey. Pytheas had no idea exactly how long. He'd follow the tin road, he'd follow the amber road. He had read all he could about the detailed world, and all the general theories of the cosmos (the water of Thales, the fire of Heraclitus, the mathematical music of Pythagoras). The Mediterranean was pretty clearly contoured in his mind, from Iberia to the Black Sea. To the south-east were Ethiopians and

Indians, to the north-west, Scythians and Kelts. The Mediterranean opened out on to the Atlantic, named after the mountain god Atlas, who, as Homer says, 'knows all the deeps of the ocean waters.'

Pytheas was the first to take a long enquiring look at the Atlantic coast of Europe. He almost certainly did a thorough study of the tin-mines of Cornwall. He was intrigued by the tides of Scotland's west coast, as he had been by those of Armorica. He set up his gnomon on the island of Lewis and made an astounding calculation of latitude. He says (quoted by Pliny) that there are forty islands in the Orkneys, which means either that he actually counted them as he sailed among them, or that a Scotsman (maybe a crafty Pict from Aberdeen) told him so.

All this would have been enough for many a bold man. Enough to go back to Marseilles with and get the city's gold medal. But Pytheas went on, alone, in silence.

He went on up to Thule, which, as Ultima Thule, was to be a theme of conjecture and imagination for centuries, and become a metaphor for the furthest reaches of possibility.

Up there in the mist and haar, feeling a world breathing in the vast icy emptiness of the ocean, he spoke of a 'sea-lung' (*pneumon thalassios*), like some great jellyfish undulating medusively in the void.

This is where Pytheas hits not only the farthest speculations of cosmology, but the most farout poetics. That, ultimately, is what has always drawn me to him, that is also (beyond all commercial, anthropological, geographical motives), what keeps me coming back to him.

Pytheas is one of the most significant, and at the same time one of the most obscure figures on the horizons of geography. And his book *On the Ocean (Peri tou Okeanou)* is one of the great lost books of the world.

Few there were who read Pytheas's work, composed probably around 320 B.C., after years 'on the ocean', in a villa overlooking the Old Harbour of Marseilles. But those who did read it made good use of it. It wasn't only a mine of information, it was a new conceptual map, and it abounded in original perceptions, sharp calculations. Of course, there were those who denigrated it (the jealousy-ridden Polybius and the squint-eyed Strabo) because it opened up space inconceivable to them, and who dismissed Pytheas out of hand as an upstart. But others, about twenty significant writers in all (among them Pliny the Elder, Eratosthenes of Alexandria, and Hypparchus the astronomer) quoted large chunks from his book in their own works, thus saving it at least in part for posterity.

So that the name of Pytheas has become a reference for anyone even remotely concerned with world-opening.

I spoke earlier of the interest of original documents. In the Scottish context, they are few and far between. But there are a whole host of documents – Pytheas and Avienus among them – coming from elsewhere that have a direct bearing on the Scoto-Atlantic context, bringing in breadth and breathing. They are rarely referred to, and if they get on to university courses, it's mostly only for secondary, tangential reasons. Whereas they could be strong, far-carrying elements in a really cogent, outlooking, far-seeing cultural curriculum.

2. AT ULLI'S PLACE

Let's look now more closely at Scotland, following the evolution of our proto-Scottish *strandloopers*.

I'd like to be able to say that we're gathered here today at the Ulla Pool. That would give us an immediate geographical location and a handy geopoetic connection. But, as you certainly know, the etymology of the place name is not geographical or topographical, it is proprietorial. What Ullapool originally meant in all likelihood is 'Ulli's place'– from the Scandinavian *bólstadr*, homestead.

Who Ulli was, and how he lived, what he thought, it is difficult to say. That's because of the scrappiness of our evidence and the paucity of our documents – so many of the Scoto-Atlantic archives have gone with the wind, been burned, or buried in the sand.

The result is, Scotland is impoverished in background.

Even where recorded history is concerned, the country suffers, despite a historicist tendency in the culture and masses of communitarian memoirs, from chronic amnesia. Otherwise, how could it take pride in a corny cultural production such as the film *Braveheart*, which, if I remember rightly (I walked out in the middle of it, in lonely protest), has William Wallace, a Welshman, as his name indicates, from Strathclyde (a descendant of the ancient Bretons of that area), prancing about with his face painted blue like a second century semi-puggled Pict. A total distortion. But Scotland has got used to that, it's been raised on that kind of stuff for centuries. Sir Walter Scott, the 'Wizard of the North', started it, telling his Tory stories in the guise of Scottish history.

If London, that congested centre, is packed with archives, it is very difficult to know exactly what was going on around the northern edge, and get into that floating reality.

I repeat: we need fresh discovery, radical thought, and strong expression – based on original documentation wherever and whenever we can find it.

With regard to Ulli's situation in Pictland, maybe some time before, or some little time after, the union of the Picts and the Scots under Kenneth mac Alpin in 843 (at which time the name Alba, hitherto used for the whole island, came to designate specifically its northern part, Scotland), the main original documents at our disposal, written in rough Gaelic and rocky Latin, are the *Iona Chronicle* (once we've winkled it out from the *Annals of Ulster*), the *Duan Albanach*, Adomnán's *Life of Columba*, the *Annals of Tigernach*, Bede's *Historia Ecclesiastica*, and the *Senchus Fer n'Alban* ('The history of the men of Scotland').

The Scotland evoked here is that enclave of the Irish Dál Riata in what was then Pictland and Breton-land, a territory that stretched from the tip of Kintyre in the south to Ardnamurchan in the north, and from Tiree in the west to the forehills of Druim Alban (which Adomnán calls 'the backbone of Britain', *dorsi montes brittanici*) in the east. They were a tough lot, the Dalriadans. Their very name suggests it. It stems probably from the Indo-European root **reidh*, which would indicate they were the roaders, the riders, the raiders. If I had been a Pict or a Breton, I would not have looked without qualms upon their arrival on Kintyre under Fergus Mór around 500 A.D. As the *Senchus Fer n'Alban* puts it, they 'grabbed Alba' (*gabsat albain*).

The sixth, seventh and eighth centuries saw their establishment and expansion.

In their policy of expansion, they occupied more and more mainland and islands ('Jura' may be from *deorad*, outlander, stranger), they fought with the Picts, the Bretons of Strathclyde (the Gwyr y Gogledd, the 'Men of the North', that is the Northern Welsh, who were in close touch with Powys and Gwynedd in North Wales), the Angles of Northumbria, and the Saxons from down the road. The chronicles and annals are full of wars, battles, torturings and drownings (not accidental, executional). As to the *Senchus*, it is to all intents and purposes a geopolitical text, establishing the relations between the Dál Riata of Scotland and Ireland, laying out genealogies and pedigrees, and setting up, in the new colonial territory, a system of civil, military and naval administration that was soon to prevail, with some resistance, over the whole country.

The Dalriadians brought over with them from Ireland the system that prevailed in the Irish tribe, or *túath*. In the *túath*, there were two grades, two classes of freeborn: the *grád flatha*, the nobles, and the *grád fhéne*, the commoners. It was the nobles that marshalled the hostings, lead the sea-expeditions, in other words, made history, while levying taxes and enforcing obligations. The *Senchus* lays these out in detail: every householder ('every house that emits smoke', as a later text said) was liable to service in the hostings (*slógad* – sluggings with slogans), and every unit of twenty houses had to supply a seven-bencher (a boat with seven oars a side) for warfare on the sea. Theoretically, you could stay outside the system. But that meant being, literally, outlawed. To survive outside, you had to form a band, a *fian*. That's what Finn and the Fianna did – but that's another story.

Ulli, not to forget him, was probably a Norseman from the Inchegal (the 'islands of the strangers', under Norse rule) who had decided to settle on the mainland, and who found himself involved, willy nilly, in all this. It would be no great surprise to him. His bunch had already done a lot of fighting, and the Norse on their arrival in the Western isles had taken over the Gaelic tax-system as they found it.

So much for the socio-political and geo-political context of Scotland's beginnings.

But something else was going on within the island monasteries.

3. THE PELAGIAN INSPIRATION

In his *Historia Ecclesiastica* (eighth century), Bede refers to events of the mind taking place 'in the western parts of Britain' (*in occiduis Brittaniae partibus*), that is, the area stretching up from Devon and Cornwall to Strathclyde via Wales, Ireland and Galloway, evoking in particular its 'northern limits' (*septentrionales fines*), the western highlands and islands.

A strange wind-of-the-spirit had been blowing over that territory for some time – ever since, after studies under Martin of Tours, in France, Ninian had returned to Scotland, to his native Galloway, where he founded Candida Casa, 'the white house'. But if the White House was a focal point, there were more or less isolated Ninianite communities all over the territory. In the sixth century, Columba founded his community on Iona, but monks made off from there (in their heads old pagan poems about the search for the perfect island, with 'white rocks by the seashore') to islands as small as possible – like Coinneach, who settled on a minuscular island off Mull, known ever since as Inchkenneth. The wind-of-the-spirit I evoked was a Christian wind, but of a highly unorthodox and idiosyncratic nature. The peculiar nature of this inspiration came largely from the thought of the Breton monk Pelagius ('he of the sea'), who coolly denied the theory of Original Sin which had become, via St Paul and St Augustine, the mainstay of the church, and was to leave the western mind in a hypocritical mess. For Pelagius, nature was not to be condemned, you just had to work at it. Maybe, behind Pelagius's thinking, there was a kind of abstract Celtic paganism – by 'abstract', I mean that it had got rid of gods and goddesses, but retained the essential: the delight in nature, and the respect for learning. It was this pelagian naturalism, and the quickening of the intelligence that went with it, which, in the wake of Pelagius's root unorthodoxy, made Clement of Rodel on the isle of Harris wonder if celibacy was such a good idea, while others had doubts about the value of baptism, and others again criticized the prayer of supplication ('Please God, grant me this, grant me that, help me in this way, help me in that way'), saying that not only was it a waste of time, it was an insult to God, who had more fundamental things to be thinking about and getting on with. If they had their own thoughts, those Celtic monks also had their own methods, almost Tibetan in their extreme austerity: standing still for hours on end with arms outstretched, in the shape of the cross; standing up to the neck in ice-cold water chanting psalms . . . As to learning, *studium*, they delighted in writing texts that brought in, with ingenious combinations, all the languages they had at their disposal: Celtic (gaelic or brythonic), Latin, Greek, Hebrew. So much so that when, later, they started swarming over the continent, they took a vast amount of learning with them, becoming, as Renan of Brittany was to say, 'masters of language and of literature to all the West'.

These monasteries were peopled by individuals who called themselves at various times *magister* ('master'), *pontifex* ('bridge-builder'), *philosophus* ('thinker'), *anchorita* ('hermit'), or *peregrinus* ('traveller'). They were indeed masters of learning, literature and language. They built a bridge between the ordinary workaday world with its pressures and perils and 'another world'. They were working at systems of thought, and working out a new thinking. They transcribed documents. They had a strong attraction to the hermit life, and they did a great deal of travelling. Their annals make mention of this or that *bellum lacrimabile* ('tearful war'), they record the attack of Angus, king of the Picts, on the Dalriada country (*Oengus mac Fergusso rex Pictorum vastavit regiones Dail Riatai*), but they also bring in 'a big wind' (*ventus magnus*), or an earthquake (*terrimotus*) on Islay, and Bede has en eye to geography, speaking of the *sinus maris permaximus* ('the huge gulf of the sea') that stretches eastward into the land as far as the *civitas Brettonum* called Alcluith and later Dumbarton.

I mentioned the fact that they did a great deal of travelling. Adomnán's *Life of Columba*, which concentrates on the Colomcillean monastery on Iona (described by Bede as the one that 'held the torch in all the lands of the northern Scots and Picts') refers again and again to movements between Iona, Tiree,

Jura and Colonsay and further away to Ireland and the Orkneys. In fact during these early centuries, the sea-traffic among the islands and along the coasts was amazing. Most sea-terms in Gaelic are derived from the Norse - the one exception is *ràmh*, 'oar' (the same as one finds in the French word *rame*). All the people living in those areas were rowing like hell, in boats composed of wooden frames covered in hides and, later, tarred canvas: curachs, coracles (latin: *curucus*). King Brude of the Picts had a fleet capable of carrying his sway as far away as the Orkneys. Gildas, in his *De Excidio Britanniae*, describing the naval expeditions of the Picts and Scots against the Romano-Bretons in the fifth century, says they came in 'a host of black coracles'. The monks travelled the same way. But whereas the chiefs were looking for conquest, the monks were looking for what they called a *desertum*, a place where they could live in isolation, surrounded by a great vastitude of waters in which they could hear God roaring like the wind and the spirit crying like a gull.

Perched there on their western rocks like birds themselves, they suddenly began to move further afield, flying in a great apostolic migration, their heads full of grammar and geography, verb tenses and tempests, quick thinking and poetry. Columbanus leaves for the Continent with twelve companions: hair worn long, shaved in a half-moon shape above the forehead; pilgrim staff in hand; bell in belt; on their backs, bags full of books. They cross Brittany and the whole of Gaul. Gibrian moves towards Châlons-en-Champagne, Malcallan to the Ardennes, Concord to Chambéry, Fiachra to the Brie country, Fridolin to Burgundy. There were so many of them at Péronne in

Picardy that the town was known as *Perrona Scottorum*. Everywhere, they set up schools for teaching and *scriptoria* for the writing of manuscripts. Sedulius Scottus at Liège writes texts in Latin and Greek, mingling prose and verse, moving without a halt from a study of the Church Fathers to a study on Porphyry, the neoplatonic philosopher, a disciple of Plotinus. John Scot at Laon translates from the Greek (notably the *Pseudo-Denys*) and creates a vocabulary that will enable minds to elaborate new thought for centuries – I've seen him described as 'one of the most solitary minds the West has ever known'. Within the ecclesiastical intelligentsia of the time, some received them with wonderment and admiration, such as the bishop of Auxerre: 'Braving the sea and its dangers, practically the whole of Scotia is crossing over to our shores. The more a Scot is learned, the more he wants to travel.' But others, predictably enough, were irritated: St Boniface couldn't thole those Scots who refused to stay in one place, and seemed to be ubiquitous. While others again, ensconced in comfortable niches, experienced the new inspiration as an unwelcome draught: 'Who do they think they are', said a bishop whose name I have forgotten, 'those Scots with their allies the Picts and the Britons, who dare to disagree with the whole world!'

Opposition gradually grew and the established Church was finally able, in the seventh century, to stamp out the nomadic network. The Celto-Christian movement was absorbed into the great orders. But even then, an underground, more diffuse influence still remained, maintaining a whiter current in the muddy flood of literature and culture. You can see it in André Breton (who salutes Pelagius in one of his poems: 'Pelagius, your

39

head erect among all those lowered brows'), in Blaise Cendrars, in Gerard Manley Hopkins, maybe even in T. E. Lawrence.

Here we come to poetics.

4. ATLANTIC POETICS

Out of the writing-places (the *scriptoria*) of the monasteries came many a poem, often with a strong Atlantic feeling and surge.

I'll mention here only two: *The Voyage of Brandan* and *The Voyage of Bran.*

The earliest manuscript known of the *Voyage of Brandan*, written in Latin, dates from the eleventh century, but there may have been manuscripts before that, and the composition of the poem may go back still further, even to Brandan's own time, the sixth century. The *Navigatio Sancti Brandani*, one of the most striking and influential poems of the Middle Ages, recounts the seven years Atlantic travelling among the Hebrides, up to Iceland, maybe down the Atlantic as far as the Azores, of this monk born at the end of the fifth century, who had founded the community of Clonfert in Ireland, but who later abandoned himself to 'the winds of God', sailing over wide seas and seeing marvels: a crystal church (an iceberg), and a burning mountain (a volcano), coming across 'an island that smells of apples', with always a certain amount of exaggeration and humour: he has breakfast on a whale's back, and in one lonely part of the ocean he meets Judas, up once a year from hell to have a breath of fresh air.

The manuscript of the *Immram Brain*, 'The Voyage of Bran to the Land of the Living' (to quote Kuno Meyer's translation) also dates from the eleventh century, but again may go back farther, and in any case is situated culturally further back. The *Voyage of Brandan* is Celto-Christian and is shot through with a rabelaisian kind of humour. The *Voyage of Bran* has a pagan otherworld eeriness to it, while carrying, like the Brandan, the whiff of real sea-voyages. Bran is walking on the shore when he hears music behind him. He looks round, but the music is still behind him (it comes in fact from 'the big stone out of which arise a hundred tunes'). He falls asleep. When he awakes, he sees a silver branch with white blossoms. He picks it up. At this, a woman appears, strangely dressed, who sings fifty stanzas of the poem, which tells of an island far away, 'encircled by clear sea', indeed of many islands: 'There are thrice fifty islands far away on the ocean to the West of us.' Bran sets out the next day. After two days and two nights, he meets Manannán, son of Ler, the embodiment of oceanic reality, who sings another thirty stanzas, about 'the beginning of creation' and about someone who one day will 'relate mysteries in the course of his knowledge' and 'be in the shape of every animal, both on blue-grey sea and red land' – he will identify with stag, salmon, seal and swan. Bran sails on, to the Island of Women where he stays for years, in great joyance, before returning home, where no one knows him, so much time has passed.

One is grateful to the editors of these texts. But one can hardly stop at erudite editorship – not if one is to continue such voyaging into other areas. One has to undertake *extravagant* research.

One has to see these vision-voyages in connection with the vision-voyage in the *Gilgamesh*, which goes back a thousand years before Homer: the journey to the Faraway Place, 'at the mouth of the river', in the ocean. One has to put them in parallel with the voyages of Scandinavian tradition: the journey of Erik to Odinsaker, the 'land of living men', in *Eriks Saga Vidförla* ('The saga of Erik the wide-faring'), which ultimately goes back to the shaman journey. Into the Bran and especially the Brandan poem comes the Christian search for the Garden of Eden as well as the peregrine search for a hermitage: a *terra deserta*, a *desertum marinum*, a *herimum in oceano*. And it's there we hit upon real local voyagings, the *immram* (latinised as *imbi-ramus*), a 'rowing about' (like the Australian 'walk-about') from island to island within the Hebridean archipelago, as well as longer journeys further out west, across the uncharted Atlantic towards America.

It's also possible to probe it all back to a radical root: Bran means 'crow', and the name of his father, Febal, is close to the Welsh *gwefl*, meaning 'lip', and 'the lip of the land', that is an estuary. The primal, radical vision is of a bird flying into the open, and thereafter, earth and sea talking, with the music of rocks and the clash of what the Scottish poet Alexander Hume (1550-1609) calls 'weltering waves'.

That's an interesting word, 'welter' – it indicates a multiplicity of elements that precedes a world, and which, in one way or another, a world has to maintain if it is not to degenerate into ideology, habit and chit-chat.

It's such a wild welter one finds in the Welsh-Breton world-bearing poems such as those of Aneurin, Llywarch-Hen, or

Taliesin, some of which may have been composed in Strathclyde: 'His horse came from the ford in the Clyde, at the end of the river', says Aneurin (even if it's not the same Clyde, the application is valid). More deeply, there was mention in the Bran poem of one who 'will reveal mysteries in the course of his knowledge' and who will 'be in the shape of every animal, both on blue-grey sea and brown-red land'. That's exactly what we find in these poems, where the mind is not enclosed in an identity, and where the feeling of oneself is of a focal point in a vastitude. This is a high-flying poetry full of vagrant lights. Llywarch-Hen, Old Llywarch, evokes the wind: 'the west wind from the sea and the wind on the mountain'; he evokes the coast at night: 'The night is long, bare the moor, white the cliff, grey the lone gull at the land's fall, rough the sea'; and what he calls the 'splendours' of the earth: 'ash-trees growing tall and white beside the mountain-torrent'. Taliesin says he knows 'the source of fertile inspiration, that comes from the depths'. While a river's flowing, he says, he is aware of all its length, he can feel it filling, he can feel it flooding, he can follow it as it disappears under the waves. Of himself he says: 'I've gone through a welter of shapes before acquiring my definitive form – I've been a dog, a deer, a blue salmon, a raindrop in the air, a star in the deep sky.' He salutes in conclusion the 'poet of the limits' (*vargat vard*), 'the man with bones of mist', who 'finds no solid banks' (*yscinvaen beirt bit butic clydur*). Aneurin for his part concludes with this: 'So long as there are things to look for, there will be minds to do the looking.'

Let's look now more specifically (it's been latent already in all these presentations) at geopoetics.

5. POSTMODERN ATLANTIC STUDIES

For years, I did a lot of looking along the atlantic coast, from Cape Breton in South-West France to Cape Wrath up in our North-West, thinking of these inlookings and outlookings as 'Atlantic studies'.

I put a lot of meaning into that word 'Atlantic'.

It referred in the first place and the first instance, of course, to sheer geophysical space – to the Atlantic Ocean, one of the great gulfs of the world ocean, stretching from North to South, and the only one to receive the cold waters of the boreal North. Its extent prolonged by the Caribbean, the Gulf of Mexico, the Sea of Greenland, the North Sea, the Baltic, the Channel, the Irish Sea, the Celtic Sea. Fed by rivers from Europe, Africa, America and Northern Asia. With a highly fragmented coastline, and with a varied multiplicity of islands: the British Isles, with their Hebridean and Orcadian archipelagoes, Ireland, Iceland, Newfoundland, the West Indies, the Bermudas, the Azores, the Canaries. Having a very complex submarine topography, with underwater ridges and sea-mountains and abyssal plains. With the Franco-British plateau prolonging now undersea the great northern plain of Europe, subjected over the ages to folding after folding – where the Rhine flowed with all its powers, gathering in a multitude of waters from Elbe, Ems and Weser in the East, from Tweed, Forth, Murray, Tay, Thames and Humber in the West. Rife with sediments and erosions. Full of complex currents ('to navigate these waters is a real poem', said a Breton seaman to me once), with much stratification of waters all bearing different salt-densities. A place of migration, both of fish (the short migrations of the sardine, the herring, the mackerel;

the long migrations of the tuna) and birds: gull, petrel, cormorant ...

Sheer physicality. The bottom line. A sense of space. And materials, movements, animation within that space.

But the sense I gave to the world 'Atlantic' didn't stop there. Denis Diderot says somewhere in one of his extravagant essays that poetics is out for something enormous. That word 'enormous' I understood in two ways: one, as immense, the other, as outside the norm. And there my Atlantic reference was to that huge compendium of notes by Leonardo da Vinci known as the *Codex Atlanticus* (*Codice Atlantico*), packed full of observations concerning, eminently, flight and flow, wave and tide, wind and movement, all these observations leading up to what was never constituted, but which was magnificently sketched, and that I thought of as a 'wave-and-wind philosophy' – like Heraclitus, but with more facts. 'He moves in the whole space of the mind's powers', says Paul Valéry of Leonardo (*'Il se meut dans tout l'espace du pouvoir de l'esprit'*) in his introduction to the French translation of MacCurdy's edition.

There was a still further sense I gave to the word 'Atlantic'. This is where that much ill-used and much-maligned word 'postmodern' comes in. Where I first came across it, and I think in fact it was its first usage, was in the last section of Arnold Toynbee's *A Study of History* (which I read as a student in Glasgow), a section entitled 'The prospects of the Western civilisation'. In Toynbee's history-wise eyes, these prospects are not bright. At the end of modernity, cultural impetus has run out, leaving room only for what one might call a cultural production without culture. And yet ... some possibility might remain. There might be a *post*modernity. If it were going to be more than a mere pile-up, mere flotsam and jetsam from the past along with fast-made, fast-consumed and fast-rejected products of the contemporary present, it would be a difficult area. Calling the man who is aware of this situation but who wants to keep moving the 'Western pilgrim', Toynbee likens his exploration to the move of those 'Phocaean seafarers' I evoked earlier in this lecture, moving out from the defined Mediterranean into the unknown and risky waters of the Atlantic. If late-modern society was strictly techno-economic, 'demonically acquisitive', says Toynbee, a postmodern culture might arise out of 'a transfer of energy from Economics to Religion'.

If I could go with Toynbee's reading of history and his analysis of a situation, I could not accept his solution to the culture question. Even if by religion he meant something more than the established church recommended by Eliot (in his *Notes towards a Definition of Culture* and other essays) – in fact he seemed to opt for some kind of Franciscan spirituality – I could see nothing at all to attract me in that direction, and nothing at all that might be the basis of a live and enlivening, founded and grounded culture.

That's why I had to continue my historical investigations elsewhere, notably in the work of Leo Frobenius.

In *The Destiny of Civilisations*, Frobenius distinguishes four great periods in the evolution of human culture: the mythic period (concentred in South-East Asia and the Pacific), the period of the great religions (Western Asia and Eastern Europe), the philosophical period (Greece), and, then finally the techno-economic period, concentred in the North Atlantic.

Up to there, the analysis is pretty close to that of Toynbee. But there is a great difference in the attitude and the proposals. For Frobenius, if techno-economic civilisation is culturally rundown, it has, by encircling the globe, re-introduced, beyond national divisions and identities, the question of *world.* And it is at the end-point of civilisational evolution, on the North Atlantic rim that, not only would the sharpest criticism of techno-economic civilisation in its end stages be made, but that a new world-thought, world-thinking, based on a new 'seizure of reality' and renewed creative energy, might come into being.

It is I who say 'might', preferring to think in terms of possibility rather than of prophecy. I also left aside Frobenius's pangermanism, as well as some aspects of his *paideuma*. But the necessity of a new *paideuma* (creative teaching, culture-basis) was something I wholeheartedly, wholemindedly, agreed with.

I was reading all these historical analyses in Glasgow, a place-name in which I read an ending (*glas* is the French for 'knell', as in 'for whom the bell tolls'), and a beginning (*go*).

The field work meant moving along the Atlantic edge, first on the west coast of Scotland, later extending that area to the whole of the Atlantic Arc. Walking the coast. Coursing among the islands. Recovering lost wavelengths.

The study work meant trying to re-discover hidden cultural channels – pelagianism, for example. Delving into old texts, of which I've given several examples in this lecture. It meant also reading more recent texts, often in a highly selective way, looking for moments of 'Atlantic sensation'. Stevenson's *The Master of Ballantrae*, for example, situated at least for its start on the

Ayrshire coast, is mostly superficial, and sometimes ridiculous, fiction, but every now and then R. L. hits the Atlantic note, leaving plot and psychology for strong and fine world-lines: 'The road lay over moorish hills, where was no sound but the crying of moor-fowl in the wet heather and the pouring of the swollen burns.' If Stevenson at his best knows how to 'keep the sea in the North Atlantic' and move out beyond his fiction ('It is no very difficult thing to cast a glamour on a little chip of manhood not very long in breeches'), I found similar things, indeed in greater quantity, in Chateaubriand, who, in his *Memoirs*, calls himself a 'pilgrim of the sea', a 'friend of the waves', and in Hugo, in particular in that great Atlantic book entitled *The Toilers of the Sea* or in the compendium of notes he called *Ocean*. Scattered signs of Atlantic genius.

Study work meant also gathering information, in as synthetic a way as possible, from the sciences: physics, biology, geography, geology, linguistics. I say in 'as synthetic a way as possible' – something which, within science itself has been called within recent years interdisciplinary, transdisciplinary thinking. Not only as multiple approaches to any one problem, but as if the sciences were trying to get back beyond, over beyond their divisions, and re-constitute something like a whole science. And poetics seemed to me, ultimately, the most synthetic language conceivable.

In philosophy, after Nietzsche's analysis of culture and his efforts to overcome nihilism, I looked to Husserl's phenomenology and Heidegger's attempt to move out of metaphysics and into the field of what he called 'beginning thinking' (*anfängliches Denken*). Also to radical critiques of humanism, such as one can find, for example, in Foucault's *Words and Things* (*Les Mots et les Choses*), where the present conception of 'human being' is likened to a face drawn in the sand at the edge of the tide, soon to be washed away. A notion which, in my mind, tied in with the biological conception of the human being as 'open system', which again tied in with certain far-Eastern conceptions of human being (ultimately identified with totality, as in Brahamanism; non-existent, as in Buddhism), and with notions of human being as vehicled and evidenced by certain Celto-Atlantic texts, some of which I have already quoted in this lecture.

Concomitantly with these investigations, I was working out my own concepts: supernihilism, chaoticism, littorality, etc., beginning a series of earth-itineraries, territorial peregrinations that I was going to write up in what I called *waybooks;* generally building up a body of work I thought of as *opus atlanticum*, and which came across in books with titles like *Atlantica* or *Atlantic Latitudes*.

It was all this, and more in the same vein, that was to lead to the theory and practice of geopoetics. It could in fact be said that for me the Atlantic shore was the threshold of geopoetics, and is still its principal location.

For years I walked this coast with the blue books of the British Regional Geology put out by the Institute of Geological Sciences in my rucksack.

Our North-west is lewisian-torridonian territory. It's the lewisian gneiss that gives that grey, glowering, hillocky rock-landscape with its boggy pools, its cotton-grass and sphagnum moss, its bracken and rushes, with, here and there, a clump of small-leaved birch or red-berried rowan. Before it got there and began to erode, that gneiss travelled a long way, from near the base of the earth's crust, undergoing multiple metamorphoses and upliftings. Till there it lies, with dark lodes of volcanic rock cut through it, to be lived with, to be looked at, to be thought about. I spoke earlier in this talk about the lack of early documents in Scotland. Well, here is one, the most original of all. In a text of 1896, 'The Geology and Scenery of Sutherland', Henry Cadell has this: 'A hand specimen of gneiss resembles a closed book with chapters of varying lengths, each chapter consisting of pages of a different tint.' The irregular stripes and bands, the inclusions and intrusions, the facets and the thrusts, do indeed invite a reading in terms of scientific knowledge, but what they provide back of the knowledge is a deep, a strong earth-sense.

Atop of the lewisian rock lies the old red torridonian sandstone that has left, where not totally eroded, those red piles in the grey desert that are Suilven, Stac Pollaidh, Canisp, the Quinag and Cul Mor. If the oldest lewisian goes back some three thousand million years, the Old Red goes back at least eight hundred. But again (though they can help in the process) it's not the dates that ultimately matter, it's that sensation of fundamentality.

With that sensation of fundamentality goes a sense of deep intercontinental connexion. The gneiss of North-West Scotland stretches over into Canada – the Caledonian chain connects with the Appalachian. This part of Scotland is, at depth, a part of the old Laurentian continent that has changed its latitude over the last billion years. Tectonically drifting, it began near the South

Pole, moved from there to the Equator, and then further north. The Solway Firth is where the great ocean of Iapetus disappeared and where two ancient continents joined. As to the Giant's Causeway, it's the result of a volcanic eruption connected with the opening of the Atlantic Ocean.

It was with a great sensation of opening – an opening world – and also with the sense of a great work-field to be set in place, that I started up the International Institute of Geopoetics in 1989. I had several models in mind. One was the college of Sociology set up by Roger Caillois and Georges Bataille in France, another was the Institute of General Semantics founded in America by Alfred Korzybski. But back of them both was the inspiration and organisation of the Celtic monastery.

The difference, of course, the great and radical difference between the Pelagian monastery and the Institute of Geopoetics is that, while admiring the intellectual vigour of the monastery, while interested in its organisational structure, while sharing, in a broad sense, its pelagian inspiration, geopoetics harbours no transcendental belief, conceives of no 'other world'. It is strictly of this world. Its background lies neither in myth, metaphysics nor religion. It is out to begin again, from the ground up.

Our world has become so familiar, our life has become so enclosed, our mind has been so socialized, ideologized, psychologized, that my reference to the rocks, my proposal to re-begin at rock-bottom level, will seem to some not only asocial, but inhuman. I do not see our humanity as being so admirable that one cannot risk conceiving other ways of being human. I think on the contrary that humanity as we have conceived it now for some time has run itself out and that what lies on its horizon is the sub-human, with a sub-culture. What geopoetics proposes, taking geo-logics (*geo-logos*) as ground-level, is a new way of being human and of living a human life on this earth.

It may be too late for humanity as a whole – I'm willing to accept that hypothesis as a general foretelling. But I cannot let my individual life go in that direction. And I do not think I am alone in this determination. What is certain is that in this re-grounding I propose there is more real pleasure, more real joyance, than in so much of the pseudo-culture at present accumulated and accumulating.

Geopoetics breaks familiarity, and recognizes a strangeness. Beginning with the lie of the land, remaining close to the elements, it opens up space, and it works out a new mindscape. Its basis is a new sense of land in an enlarged mind.

Geopoetics is no mere poetic adjunct to society, some kind of lyrical-geographical icing on the seedy cake of reality, it is a radical reappraisal of things from which consequences can be drawn in all kinds of fields. It goes further back than most cultural projects – but it also goes a lot farther forward than most reformist or even revolutionary schemes.

It is time to conclude this Ullapoolian lecture, this initial gathering at Ulli's place, first stop in the course of this trilogy of talks on Scottish culture.

I've been talking, and will be talking further in this series of lectures, in terms of an open context, but I've also been trying to give some sign of a continuous line or tradition in Scotland.

I'm well aware that a continuous line has rarely existed in history. History has meant mostly deflection and deformation:

forgetfulness of radical open context, and curtailment, blockage of evolution from that initial ground. Scotland has suffered from this syndrome as much as anywhere, and maybe a lot more.

But without at least the paradigm of more or less uninterrupted evolution, without a model, an idea, of this kind, there can be no deep sense of culture at all, only masses of confused and largely superficial 'cultural production' within a depthless, horizonless context. Which is, of course, by and large the case today.

What is necessary at the first stage of any deepgoing movement leading, potentially, to an open and freely evolving world, is a radical, wide-ranging reconnaissance of the whole field of possibility, which means looking out beyond the sociopolitical, sociocultural context in which our minds are largely confined, and in which most discourse goes on. Most of our language is involved exclusively in this interhuman context, whereas a live, lasting, life-giving, evolving culture needs also a language connecting the human being and the universe (*chaos-cosmos*). Most of our thinking consists of commentaries on this human context, sometimes analyses of it, but never gets out beyond this precinct, never fronts the open. Whereas it is this confrontation with the open, this opening of the mind and of culture, which would renew and refresh the interhuman, sociological (sociopolitical, sociocultural) context.

That is the geopoetics project.

A HIGHLAND RECONNAISSANCE

(Inverness, October 30th 2005)

PROLOGUE

Before getting into the stride of my lecture, I want to say just how glad I am to be invited to do some 'high talk' up here in Inverness, in the lands of the Old Red, those layers of sandstone sediment left by sea or lake after millennia of stillness and turbulence and stillness again, and that lie open like the leaves of a book ('the many-folded pages of the Old Red Sandstone') in which Hugh Miller of the Black Isle saw the signs of evolution. Evolution – a concept seen by many, even geologists, in that day's Scotland, as a French notion, next door to revolution, and maybe worse, because revolutions come and go, whereas evolution goes on, if at times in a marginal or underground way.

On a more personal level, part of my family, Mackenzies on my paternal grandmother's side, came from here. And it was to Inverness that Archibald Cameron came over from exile in France in the wake of the '45 to recover some Jacobite gold buried on the shores of Loch Arkaig. I have Camerons on my mother's side and my paternal grandfather bore in fact that same name Archibald Cameron – I don't know if it's a coincidence or not. Anyway, the earlier Archibald Cameron was the last man to be hung for Jacobitism in the British Isles – the hanging took place not far from here, on Rannoch Moor.

I am, by the way, no Jacobite. But I do know a bit about exile. It's as 'Scotland's writer in exile' that I'm regularly billed here and there. Let me say right away that it's an exile without pathos. In fact it's more extension and expansion than exile. Some of the best writers and thinkers of Scottish origin have done their best writing and thinking outside Scotland, and particularly in France. I have in mind, for example, George Buchanan, in Renaissance times, David Hume in Enlightenment times and Robert Louis Stevenson in the Drifting times. It has to do with a certain wanderlust, with a continentality that is Unbritish, Unenglish, and with political-cultural contexts. But to come back to the notion of exile. I think exile is the mark of any deep and far-going creativity. Ireland's greatest twentieth century writer, James Joyce, spent by far the largest part of his existence outside his homeland, living, as he said, a life of 'silence, exile and cunning'. In exile on the Channel Islands after the failure of the 1848 revolution in France and the accession to power of Little Napoleon, Victor Hugo regretted he hadn't had recourse to exile before, so great a stimulus did it give to his work. That's the positive side. The negative side is that it sometimes entails difficulties with the home country, especially where that country has become inturned, blinkered or, no doubt worse, self-satisfied. Everyone knows the phrase about no one being a prophet in their own country. Milton gave this phrase a more specific turn, saying: 'No man is a poet in his own country.' Aeschylus, exiled from Athens, dedicated his work to Time. There's almost a law about all this, a common law. While living to the full the kind of context I've just evoked, one of the things I've been trying to do with regard to Scotland, one of the constant threads in my work and the principal theme of this cycle of lectures, is to bring in a set of *un*common laws.

I've just said that Scotland is one of the constant threads in my work. That is a regular characteristic of the writer in exile. It is not nostalgia, it is not distance lending enchantment to the view – these are the marks of *forced* exile. No, it is simply that the writer-in-exile (not passively 'exiled') will have taken with him into his exile a great deal of his indigenous culture – more, in fact, of it than is prevalent in the home country. And he will work at it, extending it, expanding it. James Joyce had more of Scotic culture in him (I use 'Scotic' to cover Irish and Scottish) than the Irish nationalists. In *Finnegans Wake* not only does he resuscitate Finn as a figure, as a culture-hero, but, stylistically, the whole massive book is an extension of those linguistic exercises practised by the Scotic monks known as the *Hisperica Famin*a, which mingled, with hilarious erudition and poetic versatility, Gaelic, Latin, Greek and Hebrew.

I lay the stress on extension, expansion, and I practise this in various ways, at various levels.

That said, by way of introduction, let's get into the territory via some cultural cartography.

1. SKETCHING CULTURAL CARTOGRAPHY

In one of his essays on logical investigation, Ludwig Wittgenstein has this: 'Consider the geography of a country for which there is no map, or only a fragmentary one. The difficulty with this is the difficulty of philosophy, where the country is language, and the geography, grammar.'

If I quote this phrase of Wittgenstein's, it's to insist on the fact that I'm talking in terms of mental mapping. Obviously, we have objective-scientific maps galore – geographical, geomorphological, geological, tectonic. But, however much I delight in these, I've been looking, fundamentally, towards something else: the shaping of a mindscape in a landscape.

A country is a physical area, a social context and a horizon of intention. For the moment, what we have by way of 'world' is only the middle section, which has discarded the physical area except as huntin' an' shootin' (and skiin') land, as decor, amusement park, vague environment, and which has blocked out any deep intention.

How much even of the primary information present in the science-maps I've just evoked has got into the 'mentality' of people dwelling in this land? How many individuals realise that the Great Glen is a fault parallel to the Cabot Fault in Canada, a gash in the earth's crust filled in by water to form the five lochs, Loch Ness at their head? How many people realise that the Solway Firth marks a boundary line between two land masses originally belonging to separate continents?

History exists with us. But you can do history without thinking *historially* (I'm using that form to give the word an original sense). Geography exists with us. But you can do geography without thinking *geographially* (same as with *historially*).

My question and questing has always been how to write world – world which, in this instance, means Scotland. That has meant long years of moving along the silent paths of history and the unseen tracks of geography. What world-living means, living with the sense of a whole world, what world-thinking and world-writing means is, in the first place, getting to grips.

Nowadays, the Highlands and Islands are a region. 'Region' is a word that rings no bell with me, awakens no deep resonance. It is a purely administrative term. Whereas a strong sense of living in a place requires a lot more than administration. As to regionalism as a cultural policy it leaves a lot to be desired. It is most often restricted, circumscribed, and is without perspective. In it, identity ideology will replace a field of creative energy. Identity ideology will drag along with it both a harping on history, and a cultural localism attached to local figures simply because they are local, interpreting their limitations as the very characteristics of the region.

In place of region, I prefer to speak of territory.

What distinguishes a territory from a region is that it has an aura, and maintains a relationship to totality, to the cosmos if you like. When Augustus, founding the Roman Empire in his *Breviarium*, divided Italy into eleven (still largely tribal) regions, he not only changed the statute of the individual (from now on he would pay tribute to central administration and be recruitable in the imperial army), but transformed the whole perception of space. His move meant not only the privileging of the urban plebs and the peripherisation of the outlying areas, it meant, more fundamentally, the loss of that aura, that cosmic relationship.

This Augustine schema has been imitated by every Empire since: the British Empire, the French Empire, and, more recently, the American Empire. And with similar, indeed identical, strategies, such as the necessity of always having an exterior enemy so as to keep the interior population under control and polarised towards imperial policy, away from any real sense of creative living *within* a territory.

What I am getting at is the augmentation of creative living within a territory, which implies a relationship to the 'great outside', a new type of politics, and a renewed conception of culture.

Let me illustrate this proposition and intention with a concrete example and a reference easily shared right away by many.

Many people in this room will have read at one time or another a book by Mark Twain called *Huckleberry Finn*. I'll ask them to recall in particular the last chapter in the book, in which Tom, Jim and Huck hatch a project to do some travelling 'over in the Territory'. We're talking from Hannibal, Missouri. The territory in question was part of that vast area West of the Mississippi that Jefferson bought from Napoleon for $15 million in 1803. Before it was opened for colonial settlement and turned into the state of Oklahoma, Jefferson considered it as 'Indian Territory', reserved as such. Which meant that it was 'outside civilisation' – that civilisation represented in Huck's mind by Aunt Sally, Aunt Polly, Uncle Silas and Judge Thatcher. Here's Huck talking to himself at the very end of the book: 'I reckon I got to *light out for the Territory* ahead of the rest, because Aunt Sally, she's going to adopt me and sivilize me and I can't stand it. I been there before.' (My emphasis.)

Huck Finn was the (puerile but powerful) spokesman for a man, Samuel Clemens, who never allowed himself to speak out, and who, except for a short period of 'roughing it' (as a roaming reporter) in Nevada, never really 'lit out' for any 'territory', but lived his life in a kind of mild, but nagging schizophrenia. He was divided between the South, whose easy-goingness he liked, but which he found ridden and rotten with romance (a romance largely derived from the novels of Sir Walter Scott), and the North, whose rationality and progressivism he admired, while finding it rank with acquisitive lust, and able to think only in terms of dollars. Mark Twain loathed the society, the civilisation in which he lived, because it warped the sources of vitality and made really creative life impossible. He got through it by means of humour, despising himself for so doing. To write in order to 'please the general public' was an abomination, and in his eyes most writers were no more than social parasites and society whores. The only human type he admired was the Mississippi pilot of the old days, 'unfettered and entirely independent', living the irregular life of the river, in intimate contact with its currents and atmospheres, and knowing a transcendence – that relation to the cosmos I mentioned. Here's Huck on his raft: 'Sometimes we'd have that whole river all to ourselves for the longest time [. . .]. It's lovely to live on a raft [. . .]. We had the sky up, up there, all speckled with stars, and we used to lay on our backs and look up at them, and discuss about whether they was made, or only just happened – Jim he allowed they was made, but I allowed they happened.' It's written in the minor, off-the-cuff mode, but it's there.

What I'm trying to get at is a pilot-poetics, a cultural pilot-project.

Here I move from Huck Finn to the Scottish Finn.

2. WALKING WITH FINN IN THE
MOUNTAINS OF THE MORNING

In his attempt to get some solar energy back into what he felt as the dingy scene of Scottish culture, Hugh MacDiarmid's slogan, a few years ago, in the times of the Scottish Renaissance, was: 'Back to Dunbar!' My own slogan, at least for a start, has been: 'Back to Finn', whom Dunbar himself evokes in his 'Litill Interlud':

> *My fore-grandschir, hecht Fyn Mackcowll*
> *That dang the Devil, and gart him yowll . . .*

But haven't we had enough of Finn in Scotland, haven't we had enough of all that hoary myth and legend?

To that question, I have two answers. Yes, we have definitely had enough of wallowing in myth and legend. But, rather than just jettisoning them, in order to engage either in thick social realism or in trivialities (which is largely the programme, or rather, the menu), the thing is, to read beyond the legend and look deeply into the myth. My second answer to the question is: No, we have in fact heard little of Finn. We have heard, *ad nauseam*, of Ossian. Indeed, after Macpherson brought out his *Fragments of Ancient Poetry* in 1760, all Europe heard of him. And it was not in itself a bad thing - it set a wild wind blowing over the powdered wigs. In Britain, the whole thing got lost in a fumey controversy. On the Continent, it carried a strong inspiration, of which one can find strains in Goethe, Chateaubriand, Victor Hugo and many others. Even politically-minded men like Napoleon were carried away, or rather carried forward, by it: 'I love Ossian for the same reason that I love to hear the wind and the waves.' There really was a strong impulse there, till it got lost in a vapory kind of romanticism.

I saw a good example of that just the other day. It was down in south-west France, at a place called Montauban, where I was doing a talk and reading. Having a little time to spare in the afternoon, I went into the local museum. Montauban was the birth place of two French artists, the painter Ingres and the sculptor Bourdelle. In addition to Gallo-Roman antiquities concerning the city of Mons Alba (Montauban in its Latin original), I expected to find examples of their work. I did. In the Bourdelle room, alongside a series of busts of Occitan poets (those Occitan or Provençal poets that, via Mistral and Denis Saurat, were to inspire MacDiarmid in his Scottish movement), I was pleased to find a bust of the Scottish anthropologist, James George Frazer, author of *The Golden Bough* and several studies in primitive religion, mythology, totemism and shamanism. In the Ingres room, the most prominent piece was a mammoth-sized canvas entitled 'Ossian's Dream' (*Le Songe d'Ossian*). On it, you see old Ossian bowed over his lyre, and in the background a pale-white cluster of spooks in armour with naked, or rather half-naked, muses clinging to them. Hard to swallow now, though it had significance in its time. As I said, a vapory brand of romanticism.

But I have a more recent example of Ossianic reference to lay before your attention, and a local one.

From 4th October 2002 to 9th February 2003 there ran, at the Scottish National Portrait Gallery in Edinburgh, an exhibition, accompanied by a substantial catalogue in English and in Gaelic: 'Ossian – Fragments of Ancient Poetry'. A Scottish artist had decided to plunge back into the fray and the spray, with, in his head, the ongoing debate about Scottish identity. In fact, 'Fragments of Scottish Identity' might have been a more accurate title for the exhibition. After a series of gloomily gothic portraits of Blind Ossian against a background of ruins and rubble, comes a portrait of Scota in the dark surrounded by symbols, which is followed by a series of portraits: Robert Burns with a predictable rose, Walter Scott with a tartan tin of cream biscuits and a soldier with a red-toory'd tammy. The centre piece of the whole gallery presents Burn's two dogs, Luath and Caesar, in front of an electric artificial fire, the dog Caesar with its paws firmly planted on a Rangers carpet (or is it towel?), the dog Luath with his paws on the Celtic Football club counterpart, the whole purporting to represent the fundamental dualisms in Scottish identity.

If this symbolistic rigmarole were Scottish identity, I think we would all be excellent candidates for suicide.

Let me make it clear. I have nothing against the artist in question. I'd even say he has talent. But talent isn't enough. For a significant art to exist, there has to be a context, there has to be a field of culture. The hotch-potch of sub-culture depicted by the artist gets nobody anywhere. It is not even worth being wryly (and maybe self-complacently) ironical about it. All anyone with any real life-desire wants to do is turn his or her back and go away.

Is this being elitist? 'Elitist' nowadays is used to stigmatize anything that moves outside the habitual ruts. Since to move out of the habitual ruts is the only way to renew thought and living, one is inclined to reinterpret the word, and use it, in a modified sense, as a term of value. And one can. In an enlightened use of the term, which goes back to root, it doesn't mean feeling that you're predeterminedly one of 'the elect'. It means simply that you have retained the faculty of choice, that you are capable of discernment, capable of value-judgements, able to see that some products are more, or less, life-enhancing and mind-expanding than others. Value-judgements are neither personally arbitrary, nor socially authoritarian. They are based on study and comparison. Like taste, they can be developed. That's what education and culture are for. If you don't have them in a society, the popular judgement runs down into populism, a democracy turns into a mediocracy, and the only values left are money values: 'good' is what sells. That's the tendency today, and in fact, more than the tendency, the established norm. Real living goes on outside it. And a real democracy means the possibility of choice for all, and the access to the best sources of life and thought for everybody.

We'll come back to these big questions later. Let's stick for the moment to Scottish identity where we left it among the cream biscuits, the Rangers and the Celtic carpets, and the ossified remnants of Ossian.

I have no intention of providing an alternative image of Scottish identity. That's because, as I said earlier, I consider that real living, real intellectual endeavour, real aesthetic realisation has little or nothing to do with identity (even less with a fixed collective identity), and everything to do with a field of energy.

The identity question is a block in the system. It's like a corn on the foot, and full of corniness. Before Scotland can really get its system in action again, before it can really get moving on its own ground, it needs, not a renaissance (there was too much identity ideology there), it needs a pedicure. It doesn't need, in the first place, an accumulation of products, it needs an analysis, what I call a culture-analysis, which goes a lot farther out than a psycho-analysis. That, along with a complete re-reading of the tradition, with selection for use.

That's the work I've been doing over the years, in ecstatic exile. Before going into that field, with its open perspectives, to abandon for good the bin of *kitsch-culture*, the mix of ossification and trivialisation just evoked, here's a piece from *Finnegans Wake*:

'All halt! Sponsor programme and close down. That's enough, genral, of finicking about Finnegan and fiddling with his faddles. A final ballot, guvnor, to remove all doubt. By sylph and salamander and all the trolls and tritons, I mean to top her drive and to tip the tap of this, at last. His thoughts that wouldbe words, his livings that havebeen deeds. And will too, by the holy child of Coole, primapatriock of the archsee, if I have at first to down every mask in Trancenania from Terreterry's Hole to Stutterers' Corner to find that Yokeoff his letter, this Yokan his dahet. Pass the jousters of the king, the Kovnor-Journal and eirenarch's customs himself no less, the meg of megs, with the Carrison old gang. Off with your persians ! Search ye the Finn!'

I hope that's clear, or at least clear enough for the purpose.

Search ye the Finn!

Finn here is Finn McCool. But finn is also end – as in, to what end, to what purpose. And end is beginning, as in 'Finnegan –

begin again', and as in 'In my end is my beginning . . .'

I began looking for the Finn when I was a youngster living on the Ayrshire coast, just opposite the island of Arran, which is an epitome of the whole of Scotland. When I was six or seven years old, my grandmother Cameron would point over to the outline of the Arran mountains and ask me if I saw the warrior. This was of course a local application of the legend more highly concentrated in the valley of Glencoe where on every summit one of the Fianna is asleep, the wind on the peaks being their breathing.

To get at what lay behind my grandmother's gesture, I delved for years into all kinds of sources.

Here's a poem from what in Celtic culture studies is usually referred to as the Cycle of Finn:

'Your song is sweet, blackbird, nowhere in the world have I heard music sweeter than yours. You, priest, would do well to listen, you can always go back to your prayers later. If you knew the real story of the blackbird, priest, you'd weep tears, you might even stop for a moment thinking about your God. It was in the blue-streamed land of Norway that Finn caught the bird you now see. And he put it in a wood of the West, in a wood of fine trees where the Fianna loved to take their rest. Finn loved to lie there listening to the blackbird sing or the stag roar. He also loved the song of the grouse, the sound made by the otter as it slips into the water, and the screech of the eagle. He delighted in the noise of the waves in the morning as they rolled over the beach of white pebbles.'

As is evident from the reference to the priest in this piece, it was composed at a time when the old pre-Christian culture was losing ground here in the North to Christianity. I've spoken and written elsewhere of this transition period in Scottish cultural history, what I want to get at now is the 'true story' evoked in the text which antedates that transition period by far.

It is no easy matter.

What is called the 'Celtic tradition' is a wild welter of material, gathered in from oral sources often in a pretty haphazard way, with mythologies, warrior-tales, potted history, rigmaroles of genealogy running alongside passages such as the one I've just quoted. If not totally forgotten in the culture, it has been marginalized, subsisting only as pure erudition on the one hand, and as legend on the other, with snatches of song in between. I'm grateful to the erudition, because without it there would be little access to the material at all, but erudition can't allow itself to be selective in a creative kind of way. As to the music, you can hear strains of it right through Scottish literature. But it is often vague, and sometimes vapid, and in any case not enough. What the moving mind wants, not content with emotion, is to have its feet moving on the ground.

What we badly need is a *grounding*.

Where the original ground of the Celts was has always been open to speculation. In the books got together by Christianised druids, or sons of druids, at the turning of the cultures, such as 'The Book of the Taking of Ireland' (*Lebor Gabala Erenn*), and in particular 'The Foundation of Tara', we hear that the Celts were children of Mil of Spain and the Greeks, that after the Tower of Babel they went into Egypt, where Mel, son of Fenius ('that's why we're called the Féné'), married a daughter of the Pharaoh called Scota. Out of Egypt, they came up the Red Sea, moved north-west, passing by the Scythians (and maybe the Finno-Ugrians), then went down to Spain, Iberia, from where they moved to Hibernia . . .

All this is pseudo-Biblical, along with bits of garbled legend.

To get at the 'true story', you have to go back up beyond the Bible. As it is said in the old poem *Fintan's Talk with the Hawk*, 'Fintan was very old – but he was not as old as the Fianna.'

I have no intention here of trying to follow the long trail in detail. But there's reason to suppose it starting back somewhere on the Eurasian steppes, and entering Europe along the valley of Europe's longest river, the Danube. As they travelled along that road, the Celts named many places, making great use of that little word 'alp' or 'alb' that seemed to indicate a 'high, white place', a place of greater density (that would later be called *finn mag*, 'the white field' in Goidelic, *gwenved* in Brythonic), and they laughed at peoples whose gods had human attributes. If they loved the things of the earth, there was also an abstraction in their heads . . .

Along that road, I want to stop at a bog in Denmark. It was in that bog was found a few years back a cauldron. Many figures are presented on the sides of that cauldron, some hard to identify. But one is certainly the mythic Celtic figure of Cernunnos: seated in a kind of yogic posture, horns on his head, a torque in one hand, a snake in the other, surrounded by animals, mainly deer. I spoke of a yogic posture. You could also think of a shaman, integrated into the animal and natural world - an idea which was confirmed in my mind when, in the 70's, I saw a stone engraving made by an Eskimo woman at Baker Lake, in the North-West territories of Canada, of an Inuit shaman surrounded by his auxiliaries. The connection is obvious.

I want now to pursue that connection further. I take Finn to be a direct descendent of Cernunnos, and an equivalent of that Inuit shaman. Finn's own name means 'the white one', which gives him a kind of sacral character (like a white shaman). And if Cernunnos is surrounded by deer (like a Canadian shaman of the caribou cult), Finn is surrounded by members of his family all bearing names (Ossian, Oscar) associated with the word for 'deer'.

Like the shaman, Finn is part integral of the community, and yet also stands somewhat apart of it. To be a member of the Fianna, a man had to renounce all clanic ties, be physically agile (excellent at running and leaping) – and know by heart 'the twelve collections of poetry'.

Now, nobody knows nowadays what the 'twelve collections' were, but what is sure is that they contained poems like this one, on the island of Arran:

Arran of the many stags, the sea reaches to its shoulder [. . .]. Blaeberries on its moors, clear cold water in its streams [. . .]. Seagulls calling to one another round its cliffs. Delightful at all times is Arran . . .

or like this one, pronounced by Amorgen when he first set foot in Scotland:

A wild sea full of fish
strong earth

clouds of birds
white hail

or like this one line so powerful in its simplicity, to be found in the manuscript called *The Annals of Tigernach:*

The wind is cold on Islay

It's much more than what was later to be called 'nature poetry', that is all too often the expression of a socialized person looking out the window of a country house and admiring the scene. It's the voice of a mind integrated into the land. It's not the verse of poets, it's the poetics of the universe.

Before beginning to lay out the main lines of that 'poetics of the universe', what I call geopoetics, let me come back a moment to Joyce's *Finnegans Wake*, which constitutes a kind of prelude to it, in that it's a compendium of human culture – with Finn (both an end and a beginning) in view. It begins with the evocation of a figure who, having followed a 'commodius vicus of recirculation', comes over from north Armorica (the north coast of Brittany) to where we are now in history, and it ends with the evocation of 'A gull. Gulls. Far calls. Coming, far!'

There you have the great wandering and the space opening, with a specific geography and significant signs.

Before going on, another little addendum. It will be said, in the humdrum centres of comment and communication, that White is at it again, with his parallel itineraries, his ingathering of symbols, and his whitenesses – the latter especially provoking ire and irritation. White, they say, sees white things everywhere! Finn the White; alps and albas, 'high white places'; Alba as 'the white country'; 'shores of white pebbles'. The enumeration is true, but my argument is not narcissistic. These white things are there, and they are written into the culture, that great river of culture that flows round the world, they are written into the language.

Even those who want to argue with me on this, secondary, point (it's the high general field I'm concerned with) are in the whiteness without knowing it.

The root of the word 'argue' is Indo-European *argu, meaning 'white' or 'brilliant'. The root is there in Tokharian arkwi, meaning 'white', and in the Sanskrit, arjunas. It's there in French argent (silvery whiteness) and in our argenteous. To 'argue' is to make clear, to make white. An argument is a whitifying.

So, it's true that I've followed a track marked with whitenesses, but it was to open the general field, the high energy field, they indicated.

3. SPEAKING OUT IN ALBAN TERRITORY

When, down in Edinburgh and Glasgow, at the time of the Scottish Enlightenment in the eighteenth century, they were arguing the toss about civilisation and culture, progressivism and primitivism, reason and sentiment, as well as a whole host of similar dialectical issues, the Highland area was very much in the forefront of debate. A lot of what was said, about the Highlands and other matters, ran down into rambling ratiocination, what some people still call philosophy, or into sentimental drivel, that some people still call poetry, but a great deal of it was cogent and clear – in fact there has been very little argumentation so cogent and clear since.

In his *Essay on the History of Civil Society*, based largely on the Rousseauist pin-pointing of a perpetual tension between individual and society, but working out a specifically Scottish terminology, Adam Ferguson in Edinburgh pointed to what he saw as a fundamental contradiction between, on the one hand, 'the production and the sale of goods' and, on the other, 'the moral foundations of personality.' In Glasgow, seeing both capitalism and industrialism brutally in action, Adam Smith around 1766 was talking about 'the disadvantages of the commercial spirit', saying that, in such a context as he saw developing gigantically around him, where the citizen is at once enriched and impoverished, lost in a multiplicity of secondary values, 'the minds of men are contracted and rendered incapable of elevation, education is despised or at least neglected, and heroic spirit is almost utterly extinguished.'

'Heroic spirit' is where the Highlands came in. They came in also when the conversation turned on the theme of 'wilderness savagery' versus 'metropolitan corruption'. Or when among the emergent culture-historians, an increasing gulf was seen as opening up between *oikos* and *polis* or what we might call, territorial ecology and economic politics.

Nobody knows exactly what Duncan ban Macintyre, who had left Glen Etive in 1767 to take up service as a polis-man in the City Guard (his 'shanks erst used to philabegs, dight in splatterdashes', as Robert Ferguson put it) thought of all this. He

73

had his keep to earn and a family to support, he could enjoy a drink with cronies (his own wife had a howff in the Lawnmarket), and he could still write laments for the Misty Corrie: 'I grieve at the condition of the grass-green corrie where I used to live, and there's many a man like me whose spirit would be gladdened if it could only be as it was once . . .' White Duncan of the Songs could be content to live out his contradictions, as so many did in his time (Robert Burns among them). But the questions raised during the Enlightenment were pertinent. Beyond all the dialectical debates, what was in the air was the question of whether there existed in Scotland the possibility of a future high field of distinctive intelligence and culture – or only pseudo-culture and caricature.

One can admire Duncan Ban's songs, and his language. Whenever I'm in Edinburgh, I go to say hello to him in the old Greyfriars kirkyard. But who nowadays, and the feeling was beginning even then, could accept the feudalism and the social sycophancy that went with the life he loved? Who could accept the bardic tradition he followed, with its praise of battles and cattle-rustling, and its rigmaroles of genealogy? Who can even share his enthusiastic delight in gunning down red deer?

The question that arose in the clearest air of the Enlightenment, beyond all the fumey debates, all the heated partisanships, all the nostalgias for ceilidhs and sheilings on the one hand, commerce and shillings on the other, was the existence of a state, a *politeia*, a *res publica*, that would be neither furiously industrial nor clannishly feudal, neither blindly futuristic nor weepingly passeistic, and that, on the shall we say 'spiritual' plane, would avoid both the vicious bite of Calvinism and the smothering hug of Catholicism, without falling into flat positivism.

This is where territory comes in.

I made an approach to it, via a re-reading of the tradition, in the previous section. Now I want to take it up again, via various *acute* stages, up into a high energy field.

The word 'territory', which I've always had a liking for – my first territory consisted of about ten square miles on the west coast of Scotland, up back of the village of Fairlie – is turning up more and more in geographical, sociological and cultural literature. It seems to mark a nerve point in today's mental landscape.

If the notion of territory has come to the fore of any thinking concerned with a live world and any writing out to do more than simply reflect contemporary conditions (I don't even stop to consider more or less fantastical story-telling), it is, I think, owing to criticism of, and reaction to, a political, economic and cultural globalism, allied to a plutocratic, indeed plutomaniac cosmopolitanism, that is seen, and most often rightly so, as levelling, all-destroying, able to think (if 'thinking' is a word that can be used in this context), only in terms of power and profit.

So far so good, at least where the criticism is concerned. But the reaction can lead into all kinds of narrow nationalism, fanatical religious integrism and restricted identity ideology. Even when the reaction does not take such extreme forms, it can come over as regional complacency and couthy localism. In the name of tradition, hunters in the Pyrenees will massacre migratory birds by the thousand with self-righteous zeal. And so on. An act that may have been valid in ancestral conditions may not at all be valid today. A re-reading, discriminatory and selective, of tradition, yes – a wholesale adoption, no.

To get beyond the local-global opposition, I suggest we think in terms of open world. Today we have to think in terms of world: there are powers (nuclear and other) that don't stop at frontiers. But to think in terms of world doesn't mean neglecting or forgetting the local. On the contrary. World, open world begins where one is. Every territory, while maintaining its presence and compactness, is open, if one knows how to read it. A very little knowledge of geology connects, as already remarked, the Caledonian Chain on the one hand with the Appalachian system in America and with a mountain line running through Scandinavia east. The same goes for hydrography, zoology and linguistics. East coast Scottish rivers flow into the Rhine complex of the North Sea which is the continuation of the North European plain. Scottish birds know Greenland and Africa as well as they know Inverness. And every language has long roots. Every human being too.

In other words, by being, large-mindedly, wide-eyedly local ('wide-eyed', that's what 'European' means in Greek), you are, naturally, global.

What I've just evoked as knowledge of territory, knowledge of terrain, ties in with ecology.

The Highlands and Islands area of Scotland is one of the most complex, most interesting, and most beautiful in Europe. A French geologist whose work I admire has said that anyone interested in earth-formation should make a pilgrimage to it. But it's no longer, unfortunately, the wild wilderness and virgin territory it was. In fact, owing to industrial ideology, merely commercial interests, and short-sighted politics, it's come in for a lot of punishment. Too many people have only considered it, apart from huntin', shootin', fishin' and skiin', as a convenient dumping ground for nuclear waste and toxic materials of various kinds.

Need I cite some examples?

On the sea-floor between northern Ireland and Scotland, there's a deep broad trench known as Beaufort's Dyke. Into it the British government has been dumping explosive and chemical weaponry and, later, radioactive waste, for decades. Some of it gets washed up now and then, visibly, on the shore, and news of it gets into the local paper. But how much of it is moving about invisibly? How much waste from Dounreay Nuclear Plant has flowed out into the Atlantic? What about America's request in 1998 to dump vast quantities of nuclear stuff in 'North Britain'? What about the great load of highly contaminated soil (well beyond the 'accepted' level of contamination) dumped in Scotland from England? What about, now the North Sea's almost pumped, the repeated seismic tests for oil reserves in the North Atlantic, which, for sea-organisms, must be like having folk banging on the walls of your house day in and day out with sledge-hammers?

But, of course, who cares about blue whales and dolphins, who cares about the arctic tern, the stone curlew, the pearl mussel, the Scots primrose?

Only elitist ecologists, who don't think of jobs, society, humanity – that's the dim-witted, short-sighted, politically blinkered and commercially interested argument.

And people let themselves be taken in.

Especially if, as was the case a few years back, at Rosyth, on the Firth of Forth, where asbestos, arsenic and mercury have been dumped into the sea for years, a 'cultural' project is set afoot. The Rosyth project was for a Leisure Park, called 'Scotland the Brave', with a show of submarines, a golf course, a presentation of ancient Gaelic culture – and, no doubt, free lessons in Gaelic.

The people let themselves be taken in . . .

No doubt they will be invited to admire some day, as art objects, the oil platforms abandoned by the companies in the North Sea, forgetful, if they ever knew it, of the ironic old Gaelic poem about piss-pots floating down the Minch.

The people let themselves be taken in . . .

Until mothers begin to find strange birth defects in their children: artery malformations, holes in the heart . . . Then they begin, at last, but already too late for damage already done, to ask questions: about land, air, and water; about pollution and contamination; about industrial negligence and administrative carelessness; about the ill effects of biotechnology and agri-business; about hidden lobbies and closed corridors. They begin to realise that humanity is part of a whole context. They begin to ask for an open, wide-spread agenda.

That's when, you might say, not only an effective ecology begins, but a real democracy.

This is, in itself, something so difficult to achieve, that it may seem premature, indeed otiose, to want to go farther. But I think it's necessary, even at the start, to have some sense of the whole way, which goes on at all levels. Then, since the present state of things is the long-term result of thought, it's in the context of thought that the ultimate action has to be accomplished. So, let's move now from the domain of ecology to a field of high mental energy, and to geopoetics.

In the year 1927-1928, the philosopher Alfred North Whitehead gave a series of lectures at Edinburgh University later published under the title *Process and Reality*. This was, on my cultural cartography, one of the high moments of mental activity in Scotland. So far as I know (but I'd be very willing to be proven wrong) it had very little echo. In fact, it would be interesting to know how many Scottish intellectuals, apart from myself, have ever heard of it, let alone thoroughly examined it.

Whitehead's *Process and Reality* is an essay in cosmology, and presents the philosophy of organism, its aim being 'to elaborate an adequate cosmology in terms of which all particular topics find their interconnections'. 'Interreconnection' is the key word. In the chapter 'Extensive connection', Whitehead calls a region, what I'm calling a territory, 'the relata which are involved in the scheme of extensive connection'. The degree of generality is high – much too high for empiricists, positivists, and social realists. But not too high for the complex workings of the world, for what Whitehead calls 'the creative advance of the world'. The documentation is immense, the argumentation cogent, and the propositions brilliantly illuminating. Whitehead is, in short, a man and a mind much to my liking. He walks the high ground, with a sense of dynamic process and synoptic vision. 'The complexity of nature', he writes, 'is inexhaustible'. He perceives the phenomena of the world, all the primary data of the senses, and at the same time he is aware of a 'potentiality', an area of power (concretized, if I may say so, by those 'mysterious quanta of energy' apprehended by Maxwell's investigations into the electromagnetic field), calling the whole 'a datum for creativeness'.

As I said, a man and a mind very much to my liking.

And yet, some years ago, I had the feeling, as with other matters I'd lived long with, that I'd gone so thoroughly into Whitehead's philosophy of organism I had come out at the other end, into, at first, I knew not exactly what . . .

First of all, there's the language question. To get at a cogent and coherent synopsis, 'words and phrases', says Whitehead, 'must be stretched towards a generality foreign to their ordinary usage'. I can go with that. I can see the need for neologisms, hyperlogisms and hypologisms, and can latinate and greekify with the best of them in order to get out of the Anglo-Saxon linguistic stew-pot. But this can be exaggerated and miss the mark. It happens often with the most demanding philosophy. Whitehead speaks of 'metaphors mutually appealing for an imaginative leap'. There's a poetics like that too. I wanted to get out of metaphorisation – without falling into the penitentiary of logical positivism. It's maybe as ultimate metaphor that Whitehead uses the word 'God'. The last chapter in *Process and Reality* is entitled 'God and the World'. This is a word and a concept for which I feel no need. I consider its use as the contamination of philosophy by theology. I like Laplace's answer to Napoleon who, after Laplace's presentation of his system of cosmology, had asked: 'And what about God'. 'Sir', said Laplace, 'I have no need of that hypothesis'.

Within the tradition of Western philosophy, Whitehead can

be seen in a line running from Plato's *Timaeus* through Locke's *Scholia*. Although I have taken more than a quick look into both (especially the *Timaeus*), my own line probably goes rather from Aristotle (the *Physics* and the *Poetics*) through Bacon (the *Novum organum*), and through Hume. Whitehead, like Plato, like Spinoza, is, at bottom, a geometer (though also, at least at the latter end, an electromagnetician). I am fascinated by geometry - fascinated in particular by the biological geometrisations of Scotland's D'Arcy Thomson. But, deep down, I probably don't believe in the possibility of a complete mathematisation of the world. There are too many breaks, too much happening in an undefined openness.

It was all this, and more (but one can't talk of everything at the one time) brought me to the theory and practice of geopoetics, which, via a synthesizing of elements from many disciplines, sciences and arts, offers an orientation for future study, research and creation, and, thereby, a basis for coherent and cogent culture in our time and space, and which, while not laying out its whole cartography (I've done that elsewhere), I've been applying here, in various ways, to the Scottish context, in order to give it both sharper contours and a more dynamic configuration.

A SENSE OF HIGH NORTH
(Kirkwall, Orkneys, October 2005)

PROLOGUE

For a title to this lecture, I hesitated between 'A Sense of High North' and 'A High Sense of North'. I finally opted for 'A Sense of High North'. But the latent, or 'occult' title (as Hugh Miller of the Black Isle would have said) is 'A High Sense of North'. I'll say exactly what I mean by a 'high sense' later.

As to that word 'North', it has a whole host of connotations.

To give it, for a start, some geographical precision. A Canadian acquaintance of mine, the geographer Louis-Edmond Hamelin, in his book *Nordicité canadienne* (Les Cahiers du Québec, Hurtubise, Montréal, 1975), distinguishes, according to latitude, Near North (around 51°), Middle North (52°-57°), Great North (58°-69°), and Far North (70°-79°). After that, you're in the polar zone. Standing at roughly 59°, Kirkwall stands at the far edge of Middle North and the near edge of Great North. That's enough to have a strong sense of nordicity or northernness without getting your nose frozen.

Taking into account a whole range of factors other than the strictly geographical, such as climate, vegetation (from coniferous forest to stony desert via tundra), economy, population, and considering the Pole as absolute, it's possible also to measure northernness in terms of polar units. On that scale, the Orkneys would come about midway.

Then there's the North as *value*. That's when it becomes really complicated, or rather complex.

In the *Abstracts* of the Canadian Association of Geographers (Thunder Bay, 1973), above the signature of C. P. E. Knuth, I read this: 'Canada's "Northern vision" of a vast resource reservoir touched with the wand of capital investment, from which pour forth production, jobs, wealth, growth and national strength, was a dream in the late 1950s and early 1960s [. . .]. A new dream has emerged in the 1970s of the North as virgin territory in which the errors of haphazard development can be avoided through consideration of sound ecological principles.'

In the North all over the world, one can see those two dreams meeting and clashing. On the one hand, industrial fishery and petrol-drilling, on the other, the Scandinavian nostalgia for the Norrland, and, say, the Eskimo sense of *nunarity* (from Inuit *nuna*, land, country).

Beyond these two dreams, outside them both, but definitely closer to the second, the norrland-nunarian-ecological dream, there is a mental process one might call northernisation, or nordification.

'Nobody goes to the North, to the extreme human North', says the poet Paul Valéry, not a Northerner by birth or identity, but engaged in a process of the mind.

I'll come back to Valéry, and the complete mind-journey, later, but as an example of 'northernisation', I choose to adduce, in this liminary section of my northern lecture-itinerary, the case of the Canadian musician Glenn Gould.

A very successful concert pianist, especially as an interpreter of Bach, Gould became so disgusted at one point (around 1964) with mere virtuosity, theatrical talent and 'musical consumerdom' that he decided to break his career, abandon the concert hall, stay away from his piano as much as possible. The dissatisfaction he felt with what was going on within the domain of music tied in with his mistrust of a tendency he saw developing in society, culture, civilisation as a whole towards the 'horribly urban and therefore spiritually restricted'. It was with all this behind him that he made his first moves up to Northern Canada and Newfoundland, out to 'examine the condition of solitude' and find therein the sources of a new vigour, a new rigour, that would be expressed in an 'un-musical music'. What Gould did in the artistic sphere 'up north' was a series of documentaries for the Canadian Broadcasting Corporation, 'countrapuntal radio documentaries': 'The Idea of North', 'The Latecomers', 'The Quiet in the Land', under the general title 'The Trilogy of Solitude'.

In this work by Gould we can see the preliminary elements of a poetics based on solitude, space and silence, only gradually bringing in sounds, human, natural, electronic, but aiming at what Busoni called 'the latitudes of a total earth art', with the North as metaphor, almost as metaphysics.

It's something like this I have myself worked at for long years, and it's the area of such investigations I now wish to explore.

At the end of this prologue, it's maybe appropriate to quote this poem I wrote years ago, away back at the beginning of these northernist explorations of mine. It's entitled simply 'North':

Way up north
where the great wind blows
he is walking

way up north
where the dawn-light breaks
he is walking

way up north
in the difficult land
he is walking.

1. NORTHERN STUDIES

My northern studies began in fact very early. That was because I was living in a small village, Fairlie, on the north Ayrshire coast, very close to the spot, marked by a monument locally called The Pencil, where the Battle of Largs was fought in 1263. Everybody knows the story. Alexander the Third, continuing the work of his father, was trying to get the Scottish State together. That meant, among other matters, trying to oust the Norwegians from the Western Isles, a task which Alexander undertook – much to the wrath of Haakon the Fourth, who decided to react. Sailing out from Bergen with a fleet of dragon-headed ships, the Norwegians came by Caithness, rounded Cape Wrath on 10th August, sailed down along Kintyre, stopping and fighting all the way, and by early October were riding at anchor in the Fairlie Roads. That's when a westerly gale blew up, causing the boats to drag their anchors, driving many of them onto the shore, where the Scots were waiting for them. This time it was the Norsemen who got the worst of it, to such an extent that their only resource was to pull out. They reached Orkney at the end of October, where Haakon, already an old man, fell ill and was laid up for weeks in the Bishop's palace, having the Bible read to him in Latin and saga stories told him in Norse, till he died here in Kirkwall on December 10th. As a direct result of this battle of Largs, the Treaty of Perth was signed in 1266: the Viking Age was over, and what we call Scotland was coming into existence.

If I've gone a little into history here, it's because that historical moment of 1263 was the point of departure for me of a whole series of investigations into northern matters, concerning, on the one hand, texts and poems, and, on the other, maps and sailing directions.

It was on a book-barrow in Glasgow that I found E. V. Gordon's *An Introduction to Old Norse* (Oxford University Press, 1927). It was in that book I made my first incursions into what Vigfusson and Powell's book of 1883 calls the *corpus poeticum boreale*, making acquaintance, for example, with Snorri Sturluson, author (13th century) of the *Heimskringla* and the *Edda*, with its three parts, *Gylfaginning* (on mythology), *Skáldskaparmál* (on skaldic style), and an anthology of poems with commentary.

In the *Gylfaginning*, Gylfi, journeying in disguise, under the name Gangleri (travel-worn) visits the hidden world in search of wisdom. There the Aesir let him in on the secrets of mythology.

As soon as he's enlightened, there's great noise, the hall of the Wise Ones vanishes, and he finds himself alone on a great empty plain and the wind blowing. That's a radical situation, *the* radical situation.

Snorri himself moved between Iceland and Norway. Once, eager to get back to Iceland but forbidden to do so by the Norwegian king, he made the statement: *'Út vil ek'* ('I want out'), and went. In its determination, in its monosyllabic terseness, in its sheer outgoingness, that short statement, 'I want out', seems to me the epitome of the whole Northern thing.

The sagas, those tales of what went on in homesteads and over the seas, are mostly bare and stark, marked by a laconic humour, a clear perception of things, and a cool transcendence of circumstance. A man looks at a mortal wound he's just received: 'Ah, I see it's broad blades that are in fashion this year.' Elsewhere, there will be crows croaking in winter air, and grey wolves padding through the mist of a forest. Mythology can come in, its humanized figures treated often with salty familiarity: 'Far from me to want to say anything bad about the gods, but that Freya is a bitch.' Mostly, however, it's elemental forces that are present: storm, frost and snow, personified as Kari, Frosti, Snaer, with a shamanistic vision of nature in the background.

As to the skalds kaparmalling in icy chambers from Bergen to Reykjavik – Harald Hardradi, Ingimar, Rognvald Kali – what most marks their work, apart from the same stark economy as in the sagas:

Destroyed the farms

there's burning in Scotland
red flames, smoking thatch

is the extensive use of those metaphors they called *kenningar* (singular, *kenning*, from the verb *kenna*, to know). For the skald, the sea was 'the swan's road' or 'the gull path'; ice was 'the North sea's mirror'; a ship was 'a beaked elk'; blood was 'the sea of the body' or, more grimly, 'corpse dew'. If, in the hands of mere virtuosos, this could degenerate into precious over-elaboration (a sword as 'the trusty fish that swims in the sea of the body'), in the hands of a strong practitioner, what *kenning* (to coin a verb) led to was a field of correspondence in which the mind leaps analogically from one thing to another:

'Our beaked elk broke the bright water-breast as it made its way under the big moon's track from the place of fish to the bay of birches . . .'

I kaparmalled that one myself.

Having tried to disengage the fundamental elements of saga-telling and skaldic poetics, we come now to travelling and to a mapping, physical and mental, of the Northern world, for me every bit as exciting.

Here's an excerpt from the *Hauksbók*, that provides sailing instructions for the North Atlantic: 'From Hermun in Norway, sail due West to Hvarf in Greenland, following the North about the Shetlands, so that they can just be seen in clear weather, but sail South of the Faroes, so that only the top half of the braes can be seen on the horizon, and thereafter South of Iceland, so that you have the birds and the whales with you.'

It's sketchy, very sketchy, but it was enough to make so many set out and see the world anew, with senses fresh.

Here's the beginning of the Greenland Saga: 'Eirik was sentenced to outlawry at the Thorsness Assembly. He prepared his boat at Eiriksbay for a voyage and when he was ready, Styr and the others accompanied him out beyond the islands. Eirik told them he was going to search for the land that Gunnbjorn, the son of Ulf Crow, had sighted when he was driven off course ...'

The sea-sagas, those poetic logbooks full of salt, wind and waves, and with a sense of wonder at new strands (*furdustrandir*) and polar bears (as in one of my favourites, *Audun's voyage*, contained in the *Morkinskinna*, 'rottenskin', volume), were based on the western roads (*vestrveger*) to Orkney, Scotland, Ireland, then vaguer places such as Huitrammanaland (which Ari Marsson touched on after six days' sail west of Iceland), Helluland, Markland and Vinland; on the south roads (into the Baltic); or 'up north', *út nordr*; to Spitzbergen, known as *svalbardr*, the 'cold edge'. You traced your way by sun and polar star, using maybe a solar compass (a gnomon casting shadow on a horizontal disk), or, later, a magnetic compass, which, unlike the solar compass (but for it you needed sunlight), was affected by magnetic disturbance. The result was, you often didn't know where you were at all. But you kept on going, on the lookout for sightings (*landtoninger*).

Let's begin to generalize a bit here. It takes time for new knowledge – primordial investigations, unedited sightings – to get integrated into the world view. When they are seen at all, they get wrapped up in previous conceptions that have become convenient and commodious, or they get swept off the board until intellectual transformation occurs and a new world-view appears.

That's what can be seen in an obvious way on maps.

If, in Andrea Bianco's Venetian atlas of 1436, Northwest Europe is fairly fully designated up to Scotia, beyond Scotia what you have is a vast, vague territory with scalloped outlines. Martin Behaim's vision of the Arctic in his globe of 1492 shows, around a perfect white polar circle, a broken mass of ghostlands described as wild, frozen, empty. On Mercator's world map of 1569, the Arctic has more definite shape, all around it the limits of Europe, America and Asia, and at its centre a black mountain. Hans Poulson Resen's 'Indications of Greenland and Adjacent Regions towards the North' is thoroughly documented, with detailed commentaries all over the place, and, as a nice additional touch, a line of driftwood crossing the Sea of Ice (*Mare Glaciale*) from America to Iceland. I've just said 'America'. But it's important to stress the fact that, at the high moment of norse-viking exploration, there was no distinction of 'old world' and 'new world', the places they saw and discovered were all part of the same hyperborean gull's-path and whale-road.

I've mentioned here some of the early Northern maps I've pored over and enjoyed, but, as many people in this hall will know, the largest early compendium of the ethnology and geography of the North was made by Olaus Magnus of Linköping during his exile from Sweden in Danzig, Venice and Rome: *Historia de gentibus septentrionalibus* ('A History of the Northern Peoples', 1555), accompanied by his map made in 1539: *Carta marina et descriptio septentrionalium terrarum ac mirabilium rerum in eis contentarum* ('A marine chart and description of northern lands with an account of the marvels to be found in them'). There you have a great welter of information and illustration, with images of Finnmark, Lapland, the White Sea ('full of all kinds of fishes and birds'), the Orkneys, the Hebrides, Scotland, Russia, Iceland and Greenland, with abundant notes on rune-writing whether it be on stone or the bark of birches, the evocation of places so cold that even wolves go blind, and whimsical remarks about reindeer-pulled sleds, all the rage in Sweden, but forbidden in Gotland, because they go so fast you *can't see the landscape*.

Seeing the landscape, sketching a mindscape, gathering together the elements of a world, that is what it is all about here. Which is why I consider these early Northern explorations as one of the principal approaches to what, over the years, I have come to call geopoetics. I'm talking about a theory-practice that starts out on the edge and that opens up new space.

Having got this length, and before going any further, what I want to do now is home in on the modern Orkneys, see what's been going on, ask some questions about Scottish literature in this context, and then move out again to a consideration of literature, and culture, in wider terms.

2. WRITING IN THE MODERN NORTH

I'm well aware that I'm treading here on local ground, which can be very touchy territory. Thickly woven with social and personal mythology, it can suddenly bristle with susceptibilities and flare up with irate reaction – perhaps especially in Scotland. But I feel the need to be intellectually honest – honest to the point of ferocity (that is the Scot in me). Honest to myself, honest to you. And my purpose in these lectures is to do re-readings, raise points, and sketch out a potential new map.

If I make these preliminary remarks, it's because, up here in the Orkneys, I want to speak, in the first place, of one who was, and probably still is, the writer most beloved in these islands: George Mackay Brown.

I knew George Mackay Brown. When I first came to the Orkneys, years (and years) ago, it was mainly to see the islands, but during the trip I also paid a visit to George at his home in Stromness. It was Francis Scarfe, who was one of my lecturers in French at Glasgow University, who had told me of this Orcadian. Frank Scarfe, an Englishman, one time sidekick of Dylan Thomas, had been stationed and billetted up here in the Orkneys during the 39-45 War, and it was he who had accompanied George during his first steps in writing, giving him hints and advice. I liked George myself. But I don't share his conception of literature. I don't think it's adequate either to the reality of the islands or to our situation.

'Nowadays', writes Brown (in *An Orkney Tapestry*), 'our western art is autonomous, private, a cold lonely kingdom. It presents us with the human condition but makes no claim to do anything about it; being cut off from labours and hungers; being the preserve of sophisticated people, a small priesthood who can appreciate and understand, they alone.'

I can sympathize with this statement, at least in part. I don't think myself great art is autonomous: I think it is based on the world-of-life (but both 'world' and 'life' can be re-examined, rethought, reformed). So, I agree with George Mackay Brown that art is not autonomous, but I know, and there I disagree with him, that the way to great art can be cold and lonely. If you want to go the whole road, you have to forego communitarian comfort, you can't stay within communal practice. While too, like Brown, I loathe empty sophistry, I consider that some sophistication of research, thought and argument is a necessary stage in any significant artistic process.

In short, I adhere wholly neither to the position Brown refused, nor to the position he adopted.

Let's go into that with more precision.

There are, in my analysis, three aspects, three levels also, to Brown's position.

On the first level, over against anything smacking of sophistication, he chooses to be naïve, stubbornly naïve – he'll be the chanter of localism, the folklorist of the pub, the chronicler of the plainstanes. This can lead him into some pretty musty corners. With regard to so much of 'local literature', Brown is perfectly lucid, and unambiguously outspoken: 'a sizeable quantity of verse is produced in the islands [. . .]. It is mostly sad stuff [. . .], lyrics like flowers pressed odourless in books [. . .], all put together without craft or wit.' But when he comes across a poem by a local poet in the Orkney dialect, he is, to say the least, because of his latent localist ideology, over-indulgent. Here, without commentary on my part, is part of a poem from a batch which he describes (in *an Orkney Tapestry*) as 'the most beautiful poems written by an Orkneyman since the Reformation killed the songs and ballads of the people':

Look ! This is Liza's but and ben
Wi' screen o' bourtrees tae the door,
Her stack o' peats, her flag-roofed byre,
Her planticru abune the shore;
Yet 'mang the hens and hoosehold gear
She's bruck'd aboot for eighty year.

Maybe, just to get things absolutely clear, I should make a
quick commentary after all: this is sub-Burns, comparable to the
worst of the worst of bad Wordsworth, and should have got no
further than the poetry column of the local newspaper. But
Brown chose to recommend it: 'the most beautiful poems since
the Reformation'. It's too much, far too much. And was in no
way likely to stimulate significant writing in the Orkneys, open
up a field of live culture in the archipelago.

Let's go to a higher level of Brown's position.

'In the northern islands December is a dark month', he writes
at the start of his chapter 'The Midwinter Music' (again in *An
Orkney Tapestry*). 'The lamps are burning when people go to their
work. Light thickens again in the early afternoon. The weather,
more often than not, is cold and stormy. There are also clear
calm nights when the hemisphere of sky is hung with stars and in
the north the Aurora Borealis rustles like curtains of heavy
yellow silk.' That's good enough stuff – maybe a bit disjointed
and metaphorically a bit hung-up at the end, but fine, and
promising. We're all ready for a sketch of winter in the North,
with something of the strength of Fridtjof Nansen's Aurora
borealis woodcut reproduced in his *In Northern Mists* (New York,
Frederick A. Stokes Company, 1911). But Brown's midwinter is
'the season of Nativity', and 'the time of trows'. What he presents

us with, in a tone of pantomime drama ('Why have the singers not been ushered inside, as in former years? Surely something evil and sinister has happened!'), is a potted anthology of christological folklore. Not quite the kind of gothic goblinism some other people go in for, but too close to it.

No doubt in saying this I reveal myself as one of those 'puritans, hedonists, humanists, democrats, pragmatists, rationalists, progressives' whom Brown stigmatizes pêle-mêle as having no sense of 'the ancient magical ceremonial quality of art' when he comes to the third level of his position (in 'The Ballad Singer' chapter of *An Orkney Tapestry*). Here Brown is militantly anti-Enlightenment, anti-Democratic, anti-Protestant (he converted to Catholicism in 1961, finding in it not only a faith, but 'a treasury of symbolism'). Again, I can go with some of his anti-ness, and, I hope it's obvious, I'm not speaking here as an anti-Catholic Protestant. What I'm getting at is the fix Brown's positioning leads him into: an archetypal, archi-hierarchical context which he conceives of as literary heraldry: 'Heraldry is the mysterious signs, deeper than art or language, by which a family or a tribe pass on their most precious secrets, their lore of a kingdom lost.' (*An Orkney Tapestry*, 'Islands and People'.) This is a very enclosed culture indeed, enclosed and quartered. I don't think it's in any way valid for us today. And I don't think it's true of the North, Orcadian or other.

The only exception to this communitarian, archetypal enclosure, the only *opening* comes when Brown takes his point of departure from the Nordic culture I presented in the previous section of this essay. I remember seeing years ago in some magazine an article in which the author said that Brown had 'an audacious sense of history', because his view of the Orkneys was not that of 'a remote offshore community' but of 'a crossroads of trade and pilgrimage'. To call Brown's awareness of the early history and culture of the islands as 'audacious' is a sign not only of the degree of ignorance one has come to expect from a certain type of journalism but also of the indigence of so much of the general cultural context in Scotland. One would have thought that by this time some sense of Nordic culture and of geographical movement in the North would be part of common knowledge. But not so. It took even Brown, cradled and educated in the Orkneys, a long time to discover the *Orkneyinga Saga*. When he did, it was, he said, like Keats reading Chapman's Homer: 'A whole new world opened up' (from my conversation with him years ago in Stromness). A lot of what he did with it is re-telling, in a primary school kind of way (and style), but some of his best poems stem from it – like, say, 'The Five Voyages of Arnor':

I, Arnor the red poet, made
Four voyages out of Orkney.

The first was to Ireland.
That was a Viking cruise.
[. . .]
Norway hung fogs about me.
[. . .]
A white wave threw me on Iceland.
[. . .]
I went the blue road to Jerusalem

. . .

But if Brown can follow Arnor on his four sea-voyages and see him through to his last death-voyage, if he can write a Viking's testament, he has, all in all, little awareness of the space and scope I referred to above, little sense of the sheer geography. In *An Orkney Tapestry*, there's a story called 'Crusader'. The Norwegian crusader and his crew pass through the Straits of Gibraltar and find themselves in the Mediterranean: 'undulating acres of blue silk' (that's not a kenning, it's metaphorical marmalade – but no matter, for the moment what I want to get at here is the geography). They put in at Narbonne in southern France, and stay there the summer. Then, instead of making their way on to the Eastern Mediterranean, which we expect, they double back to the Spanish coast (okay, so they had business there, but wanted to see Narbonne first, I'll accept that – again, it's geography I'm after). They leave Narbonne at the end of the summer and, we are told, 'arrived at the Spanish coast before Christmas'. Some going, one thinks. Narbonne is only a stone's throw from the Spanish coast. So that crew must have been very tired Vikings. Either that, or they were dead drunk and spent half their time rowing backwards.

I'll leave Mackay Brown there, 'beside the ocean of time' (the title of one of his later books – pretty awful stuff: simplistic, repetitive, childish, rank with the self-conscious complacency of 'the local poet'), midway between couthiness and Catholicity, and turn to another Orcadian writer whom I consider all in all more significant, both for Northern culture and for world-writing, Edwin Muir.

If George Mackay Brown was sedentary to the point of

chronic incrustation, Muir was a wanderer. Most people in this hall will know the broad outlines of his life: uprooted from his native Orkneys at an early age, transplanted to a Glasgow that traumatised him, later spending most of his life on the continent, between Vienna and Prague. Here he is writing in 'The Journey Back':

> *Through countless wandering*
> *Hastening, lingering*
> *From far I come*
> *And pass from place to place*
> *In a sleep-wandering pace*
> *To seek my home . . .*

It is not my intention here to follow Muir's itinerary in detail or to analyse his work as a whole, as I did Mackay Brown's, which I took as symptom and symbol of a certain Scottish situation. What interests me in the present context is to see what Muir has to say by way of analysis about Scottish literature and Scottish culture, and what future lines he would like to see. He does this in a book entitled *Scott and Scotland* (1936), but the theme of which is better described by its sub-title: 'The predicament of the Scottish writer'.

A predicament (*pre dicere*) is a crucial blockage that prevents one from speaking out adequately. This is, according to Muir, the radical situation of the Scottish writer. When he refers in his poem to 'home', Muir is not thinking in terms of some couthy installation, he is referring to what he calls elsewhere a 'completeness': a whole mind, a coherent discourse, a high order. And in Scotland he sees none of it. Scotland for him is neither a nation, nor a province (as, say, Provence once was, which developed both a high and idiosyncratic culture), it is a no man's land, with, at its centre, a black hole. In less imagistic terms, unlike England, which is 'organic', Scotland is 'an imperfectly integrated society', the psyche of its citizens marked by a divorce between sensitivity and intellect which amounts to a schizophrenia. There are obvious political and religious reasons for this predicament, and one can harp on them, but such harping will do nothing to change the situation, it will simply be an additional aspect. Neither, says Muir, and hence his quarrel with Hugh MacDiarmid, will any nationalism, or renaissance. These will get lost in secondary issues, such as the programmatic use of Lallans or Gaelic, and get blocked in the question of identity where, for example, the schizophrenia diagnosed and stigmatized by Muir, re-baptised the 'Caledonian Antisyzygy', will be reclaimed as a primary constituent of the Scottish mind.

Muir has a point there – in fact, more than a point, the thin edge of a wedge. Where I would take issue with him is on two points, which are connected. Leaving aside the question as to whether England is still an 'organic' culture, I am not convinced that 'organic' is the best epithet for a live human culture (it could mean mere embedded convention) – unless one extends the term to 'organicist' (in the Whitehead sense), in which case England was never that any more than Scotland. Then, the very fact of Scotland's 'no-man's-land' emptiness can, I think, be seen as a potential advantage: it was in an empty no-man's-land that Whitman, Thoreau and Melville developed the great original American literature.

Another reason why I do not share Muir's penchant, at least within the British Isles, for 'organic English culture', is that the separation of sensibility and intellect he finds in Scotland is exactly what T. S. Eliot, in his early investigations (essays such as

Tradition and the Individual Talent of 1919) found in England, calling it 'the dissociation of sensibility'.

Before coming back to these radical levels, let's look at the general ecology of culture within Britain, as outlined in Eliot's *Notes towards a Definition of Culture* (1948). Despite its rather stale and stodgy prose, and a propensity to hum and haw repetitively on the fence, Eliot's essay has at least the merit of stating the problem: 'It should be clear that I attempt no solution to the regional problem [. . .]. I am trying only to take apart, and leave to others to reassemble, the elements of the problem.'

While he is out to show that he is not unaware of the 'colonisation question', and keen to defend himself against a possible charge of simply representing, however diplomatically, a political-economic and cultural status quo, it is obvious that, in Eliot's mind, while he makes a plea for diversity in unity, there is, in the first and most powerful place, English culture, to which the 'other' cultures (he specifies Scotland, Ireland and Wales) are 'peripheries' or 'satellites'. While it is natural and reasonable for 'any vigorous small people' to 'preserve its individuality', he says, it will be good for that local culture to remain within the status of a satellite: 'It is that the satellite exercises a considerable influence upon the stronger culture; and so plays a larger part in the world at large than it could in isolation. For Ireland, Scotland and Wales to cut themselves off completely from England would be to cut themselves off from Europe and the world, and no talk of auld alliances would help matters.'

I agree with Eliot on the necessity for a (Scottish) culture to have contact with 'Europe and the world', but doubt very much if a satellite relationship to England would provide that. It was a direct relationship with Europe and the world, outwith the English Channel, that Scotland had before it got colonised and provincialised – a direct contact which, as lone-wolfer, and maybe cultural envoy, I have been out to maintain. As to 'auld alliances', before he had settled into the mould of Anglican unity, it was to France (to certain nineteenth century French writers such as the Breton Tristan Corbière) that Eliot himself had turned for examples of a kind of writing that would get beyond the 'dissociation of sensibility' he felt was endemic to English writing and British culture. In this early move to a culture outside a Britain anxious for its unity, Eliot is close to Europe-minded Muir, for whom 'Scottish literature lacks whole areas which are found in others' (Muir was thinking mainly there of the nineteenth century German poet Hölderlin).

Dropping here the British complex and the terms of the kind of secondary debate so many cultural programmes are made of, with a multitude of secondary creation ('Scottish writing', 'Welsh writing', etc.) as reference, what I want to get back to – the Northern tip of my argumentation (but I had to open the whole field) – is the question of world-writing, world-culture, and the constituent elements of world-making work.

'What meaning, if any', asks Eliot in his essay, 'can be attached to the term "world culture"?' The notion remains as a kind of difficult field and magnetic, challenging horizon: 'We cannot resign the idea of world-culture altogether'; 'We are pressed to maintain the ideal of a world culture, while admitting that it is something we cannot *imagine*.'

One man who did try to imagine it, working in isolation in the North of England, with a great deal of European thought at his disposal, was Samuel Taylor Coleridge. I consider Coleridge's *Biographia Literaria* to be the most interesting piece of radical literary theory ever to have come out of Britain. Certainly it is a wild and outlandish book. Arthur Symons described its content as a landscape of stones, ditches and morasses and its movement as darting forward, doubling back, and fetching wide circuits, with no visible end in view. Really original work often takes on that kind of shape.

From this outlandish book, I'll bring forward here only the distinction Coleridge makes between fancy and imagination (familiar to students of literature, but hardly ever meditated, and even less applied) and, on deepening investigation, between image and idea. The image is what strikes the senses (the more perceptive they are, the better), the idea is an abstraction – originally, as in Pindar, 'the visual abstraction of a distant object', extended by Coleridge into the action of the speculative intellect in conjunction with esemplastic power. Going away beyond the merely empirical accumulation (with subsequent classification) of observable facts, going beyond the systems of philosophy, Coleridge was looking for 'an abiding place for my reason' that would be close to 'the ground of things'.

This brings us straight to geopoetics, which of course we've been approaching all the time, catching sight of it here and there.

3. GEOPOETICS AND THE NORTH

In the autumn of 1798, Samuel Taylor Coleridge, made a voyage up the North sea from Yarmouth to Hamburg. He included his account of it in the *Biographia Literaria*, in fact it was with it he *concluded* the *Biographia*, which is to say just how much it meant to him. Here's an excerpt from it – what I take to be its culminating moment:

'At four o'clock I observed a wild duck swimming in the waves, a single solitary wild duck. It is not easy to conceive how interesting a thing it looked in that round objectless desert of waters.'

What for many would seem perfectly insignificant assumes, in the mind of Coleridge, at the end of a long bio-graphical itinerary, an importance of the first order.

It is, in fact, the primary geopoetic moment.

It is what Joyce came to at the end of the long linguistic pantomime, the cultural compendium, of *Finnegans Wake:* 'A gull. Gulls. Far calls. Coming, far!' This is what Eliot came to, in the last of his late landscapes, Cape Ann, that brought in New Hampshire, Virginia, Usk and Rannoch Moor: 'Resign this land at the end, resign it to its true owner, the tough one, the sea-gull. The palaver is finished.' This is what Edmund Husserl, after a thorough exploration of 'the crisis of the Western mind', after intense investigations into the relationship between space and thing, after long years of cartesian meditation, came to, calling it transcendental phenomenology.

Phenomenology is a nodal point in the field of geopoetics.

I've already given elsewhere a general introduction to the field of geopoetics – in the essay-book *Geopoetics: Place, Culture, World*, and in another version of the same essay contained in *The Wanderer and his Charts*. I won't go into it again here in general terms.

What I want to give is a sense of evolution within the field, switching metaphor from field to road.

Away at the beginning of this lecture, I quoted Paul Valéry, a Southerner (we are not concerned primarily, especially at this final stage, with an ethnological North), saying: 'Nobody goes to the North, to the extreme human North.'

The geopoetician (geopoetician – like mathematician, but never reducing the world to total mathematisation) does.

Before, in conclusion, giving some idea of how one writer, myself (the one I know best, as Thoreau would say), has followed the North Road into the high field of geopoetics, let's get that notion of 'extreme human North' on the map.

Where the 'extreme human North' began in the modern context, where Valéry caught on to it, was in the work of Nietzsche.

One of Nietzsche's early books, coming after the *Untimely Considerations* and *Human All-too-Human*, was entitled *Aurora*. It bore as epigraph a phrase from the Sanskrit *Rig-Veda:* 'There are so many dawns that have not yet shed their light.' Feeling that he was living in a world of confusion, trivialisation and vulgarisation (he was convinced in particular that, with its utilitarianism and empiricism, England had caused 'a general depression of the human mind'), he moved out on to what he thought of as the High North (hyperborean) Road, writing some fifteen years after *Aurora:* 'Let's face it. We are Hyperboreans. We are very well aware at what distance, in what remoteness, we live [. . .]. We know the way, we've found the way out of whole millennia of labyrinth. Who *else* has found it? Not modern man, for sure. "I don't know where I come from, I don't know where

I'm going." That's what modern man moans all the time. It was that modernity we were sick of: its pollution, its ambiguity, its compromise [. . .]. Rather live in the ice than in all that moral miasma!' If most writing, when it wasn't just telling stories for infantile or tired minds, consisted simply in comments on this or that, if most poetry was never more than potted insignificance, with no sense of the real possibilities of life, if most thinking went on in the murky labyrinths of an enclosed consciousness, this Hyperborean road meant a new type of thinking, faster, and closer to the things of the earth, and a new type of writing, again faithful to the earth, but with an unwonted amplitude and sudden enlightenings.

It's here I come, succinctly and summarily, at the end of these Highlands and Islands lectures, to my own path.

Where the hyperborean road, which turned into the intellectual nomadist road, which turned into the geopoetic road, started for me was on the shore and in the backcountry of a west coast Scottish village, amid a welter of primary phenomena. But it began to be articulate, even if it did not yet have its specific terminology, when I was a student in Glasgow, reading Nietzsche, Husserl and Heidegger, Rilke and Hölderlin, Rimbaud, Breton and Artaud – and a lot of Scottish literature.

I began to be aware of what I thought of as an Aurora Borealis of the intelligence – a poetic intelligence, thinking of those Northern lights that leap in splendiferous colours about sixty miles above the earth, and are caused by the electrons of the solar wind entering the earth's magnetic field and running along its lines into the atmosphere. The phenomenon is real – I use it also metaphorically, analogically, for a field of poetic energy and intellectual light.

My own first stage on this kind of itinerary was marked by a book of poems entitled *The Cold Wind of Dawn*. The continuity of the hyperborean, auroral metaphor is so obvious I need not comment on it. That was the threshold, the opening of the field – expressed sometimes in hyperbolic terms.

But in another book, a prose book, written at two different periods in Paris, the first when I went there at the end of my studies in Glasgow, the second after my break with the British scene, after, also, the last act of the May '68 revolt in Europe, that I went into more detail. The terms are less hyperbolic, more humorous, but the intention is the same. It's the same 'hyperborean' road. The second section of this book is entitled 'On the Hyperborean Edge', and the second goes even further: 'A Short Introduction to Eskimo Studies'. Here's an extract from this latter section: 'They still take me for a Scot. But I'm really an Eskimo, by naturalisation. In fact, even that's just for my passport – I'm a Hyperborean. Nobody knows much about the Hyperboreans. The Hyperborean is engaged on an erratic path to a far-out something. What people see are the erratics (the stones he leaves on his path), what he sees are flashes of the far-out thing.'

It's traces of that 'far-out thing' I follow in that type of literature I came to call *waybooks*. I've written quite a few of them.

All of them are concerned with that 'High North', with that high sense of North, even if they are situated in the South, the West, or the East. But a lot of them actually go north: *The Blue Road*, for example, that travels the north bank of the St-Lawrence before crossing into Labrador and ending up at the

Bay of Ungava. Another north-going book is *The Wild Swans*, that starts in the confusion of Tokyo and moves up to the northern island of Hokkaido (the 'North Sea Road').

The ultimate area of these geographico-poetico-intellectual journeys I long thought of as 'the White World' because, as High North, it was white in our physical maps, and as yet undefined on our mental maps.

But with more and more elements coming in, more and more thought being applied to them in my essay-work, and more and more experiments in poetic writing being made, I came to develop the field of geopoetics. Geopoetics is the field that opens out at the end of intellectual nomadism.

The process is ongoing and practically unending. The nomadism goes on, and the field is forever enlarged. But if there is in my life and work a continuing errancy, there is also a determined intention to establish a residence, to found and ground.

This evocation of the dialectic of errancy and residency, going along with charting and cartography, brings me to my conclusion, which is a quotation from *Biographia Literaria:*

'Grant me a nature', says Coleridge, 'having two continuous forces, the one of which tends to expand infinitely, while the other strives to apprehend or *find* itself in this infinity, and I will cause the world of intelligence to rise up before you'

That's what I've been trying to do over the years, and in particular this evening, up here in the North, the ultimate point of this series of lectures.

What we're after is a world of expanded intelligence expressed with poetic force and clarity.